Reading for Life

Why is it that more people can't read and write? Why are there still so many vastly different methods of teaching literacy? Why do people still argue about it?

Reading for Life examines these three questions, addressing the less evidence-supported ideas about teaching reading and writing which are still alive and well in schools all over the world. This accessible guide bridges the gap between research and practice, translating academic findings into practical suggestions and ready-to-use techniques.

Written in an approachable style and with informative graphics, vignettes and interviews woven throughout, this book covers:

- the components of literacy, including phonics, vocabulary and fluency
- the history of approaches to literacy teaching and an overview of the key figures
- government-level inquiries into the provision of reading and writing teaching
- the mindset which leads to acceptance of poor practice
- the essential components of an effective literacy program with practical advice on selecting resources to get the job done well

Reading for Life helps educational practitioners make informed decisions about which teaching methods to reject and select, and empowers parents to ask the right questions of professionals and policy makers. This book is a timely exploration of poor teaching methods and is an innovative, fresh assessment of how high quality literacy teaching can be provided for all.

Lyn Stone is a linguist and runs *Lifelong Literacy*, a specialist tutoring practice for children and adults with learning difficulties, on the Mornington Peninsula in Australia. She also writes courses, trains teachers and acts as a consultant for schools on matters of literacy and language.

Reading for Life

High Quality Literacy Instruction for All

Lyn Stone

Routledge
Taylor & Francis Group

LONDON AND NEW YORK

First published 2019
by Routledge
2 Park Square, Milton Park, Abingdon, Oxon OX14 4RN

and by Routledge
52 Vanderbilt Avenue, New York, NY 10017

Routledge is an imprint of the Taylor & Francis Group, an informa business.

British Library Cataloguing-in-Publication Data
A catalogue record for this book is available from the British Library.

Library of Congress Cataloging-in-Publication Data
A catalog record has been requested for this book.

ISBN: 978-1-138-59090-8 (hbk)
ISBN: 978-1-138-59092-2 (pbk)
ISBN: 978-0-429-49076-7 (ebk)

Typeset in Melior
by Deanta Global Publishing Services, Chennai, India

For my beautiful Chloe.
Always in my thoughts.

Contents

Contents

Notation guide

Standard phonemic symbols for English (RP and similar accents) have been used between slanted brackets to indicate phonemes.

Consonants

/p/ (pig) /b/ (big)
/t/ (ten) /d/ (den)
/k/ (kill) /g/ (gill)
/f/ (fan) /v/ (van)
/θ/ (thin) /ð/ (that)
/s/ (sip) /z/ (zip)
/ʃ/ (ship) /ʒ/ (vision)
/t͡ʃ/ (chill) /d͡ʒ/ (Jill)
/m/ (map)
/n/ (nap)
/ŋ/ (sing)
/l/ (light)
/r/ (right)
/w/ (wit)
/h/ (hit)
/ʍ/ (whip)
/j/ (yes)

Vowels

/ɒ/ (got)
/ɔ:/ (law)
/ɜ:/ (her)
/ʊ:/ (boot)
/ʊ/ (put)

Notation guide

/e/ (g<u>e</u>t)
/ɪ/ (s<u>i</u>t)
/i:/ (tr<u>ee</u>)
/æ/ (b<u>a</u>t)
/ʌ/ (g<u>u</u>m)
/a:/ (b<u>ar</u>)
/eɪ/ (d<u>ay</u>)
/ju:/ (d<u>ue</u>)
/aɪ/ (d<u>ie</u>)
/əʊ/ (goat)
/ɔɪ/ (b<u>oy</u>)
/aʊ/ (c<u>ow</u>)

Letter names are indicated by symbols placed inside angle brackets: <a> to <z>.

Foreword

I wish I had written this book!

Lyn Stone, with her strong background in linguistics and a deep understanding of the empirical reading research, brings a wealth of expertise to the subject of helping all students embark on the journey to independent reading. It is both a passionate and a research-based explanation of the reading process for teachers (who should have learned this at university, but most of whom did not) and for parents who are struggling to understand why their child has not learned to read. It is a highly readable analysis of the research into reading development; an honest and uncompromising reflection on years of supporting students who have struggled to acquire this critical life skill; and a practical manual for those who seek to do likewise.

The first section of the book examines different models of reading development that have been in favour over the past century, and helps the reader understand why this topic still attracts so much heated debate. It examines in some detail the five key components of reading identified by the Report of the National Reading Panel (2000) – phonemic awareness, phonics, fluency, vocabulary and comprehension – and the underlying role that oral language plays in preparing children for all literacy development.

Subsequent chapters explain, in language that is accessible to both teachers and parents, the underlying processes that have an impact on reading development: difficulties in Rapid Automatised Naming (RAN); short term, long term and working memory issues; and low processing speed. Importantly, 'interventions' and training programs purported to develop these processes and thereby improve reading are exposed, as many parents and some teachers are swayed by the claims of those beholden to mistaken ideologies, or motivated by financial gain, rather than children's reading development. And a brief but powerful chapter highlights the fact that *illiteracy is everybody's problem.* The author's professional and personal experiences have clearly resulted in a special empathy and understanding of the impact that *not l*earning to read has on individuals, their families and the broader community.

Of particular relevance to teachers is a summary table of the major contributors to the vast body of research that has informed our current understanding of the reading process and how best to teach it. Explanations of the geopolitical and social forces that have influenced broad approaches to education as well as to reading instruction make for fascinating reading and go some way to explaining why consistent recommendations from research reports have not been implemented in the English-speaking world, and the subsequent slide in international literacy rankings.

I, like many of those involved in reading research and instruction, have long been perplexed by the fact that despite the consistent findings of research over the past five decades, approaches that do not reflect this knowledge continue to be both implemented and fiercely defended. One of the ways we can counteract the spread of nonevidence-based practice is to build a greater understanding of the reading process and how it can be taught most effectively. This book will do just that.

A vast store of knowledge has accrued for those seeking advice on how to help their children or students, and this book directs the reader to this knowledge base. Parents and teachers alike will benefit from the information regarding individuals, groups and organisations that now exist to support an evidence-based approach to teaching literacy skills.

While many books about reading difficulties avoid discussion of the contentious topic of dyslexia, this one does not. While acknowledging that the word can mean different things, the author dispels many of the myths surrounding the term, including the myth that people with dyslexia can never learn to read.

The final section of the book provides practical strategies and techniques for helping the 'hard to teach' student along their literacy journey, including comprehensive chapters on teaching phonological awareness and phonics. For over 30 years I have been involved in supporting teachers to teach these important elements of the reading process (and I don't think I have done a bad job), but in these chapters I discovered new and innovative strategies I had never considered. The author's deep understanding of the sounds of English and how they are formed in addition to her knowledge of the reading process, have led to the development of strategies that deserve wider dissemination. And unlike many (roughly) comparable books, it includes detailed guidelines for teaching fluent handwriting skills (an associated problem for many children who have difficulty learning to read), and for explicitly teaching the letter names and order of the alphabet. As the author says, 'The world is alphabetised!' Children need this important information.

The chapters on teaching fluency, vocabulary and comprehension are briefer, but also include reference to valuable resources and core ideas that will help teachers and parents support these important elements of reading.

Most teachers have taught students who appear to learn effortlessly, and whose rapid achievements we herald as if they are the results of our wonderful teaching. The author reminds us, however, that, 'The mark of a good teacher or system is the output of their *bottom* students, not their *top* ones.' Fortunately, this book will help teachers raise the achievement of those who are struggling with this life skill, so that more children will enter the world of independent reading, and experience all the joys that achievement affords.

Dr Deslea Konza
PhD MEd(Hons) Dip Spec Ed B.A. Dip Ed
Associate Professor of Language and Literacy
Edith Cowan University

Preface

I'd love to be out of business. I'd love to wake up one day and make the decision to close my doors forever.

I work with children who struggle to read and write. I work with teachers, designing programs and consulting to schools on how to raise standards in reading, writing and spelling. I wish I were redundant.

There was a point in time when my ego had me believe that when a student of mine learned to read, it was somehow the doing of my own brains and personality. What vanity. I don't have any unique talent. I don't have a magic touch. It amuses me to think that I could ever have entertained such a tragic notion. I politely disagree with parents who send me kind messages about my 'techniques'.

Bringing children to literacy is not a product of *my* methods. I have some experience, I have some tricks up my sleeve, I'm fairly good at establishing a respectful, productive rapport and I enjoy what I do. But none of this actually *teaches* my students to read.

What teaches them to read is systematic, structured lessons in the relationship between speech and print and the practice that they do. They really could have received this at school. They really *should* have received this at school.

I learned how to be a conduit for this by having a degree in linguistics and by lucking into very effective training, under some of the most intelligent, well-trained mentors around.

It was luck, not shrewd insight, which put me in a good position to help children read and write. I was not immune to snake oil and wishful thinking in many aspects of my life. For instance, twenty years ago, if you had said to me that children got sick through no fault of their own, I would have scoffed at you. I would have shaken my head and pitied you for thinking that some people lived in poverty due to circumstances beyond their control. I would have been suspicious of you if you supported a family member's treatment of cancer through chemotherapy, radiation or surgery. In the back of my mind, a 'karma' type question would have lurked.

Then life hit me with a series of blunt, brutal strokes that turned a very credulous, vaguely spiritual ape into an increasingly prudent and sceptical human. It is this human who offers this book, not from a position of superiority, but of humility. I know what it's like to *think* I'm doing good when actually I'm not.

What works best in teaching *all* children to read is not a mystery. There have been many theories and models of reading and, having run them through the lens of scientific enquiry for the past 100 years, we have arrived at conclusions that point to certain specific phenomena. The first section of this book outlines those phenomena.

Even the trickier question of what can stand in the way of learning to read, and how to assist with that, is not a matter of conjecture anymore. We absolutely have that information at our fingertips and we've had it for long enough now to be doing better than we are.

So how come more people can't read and write? How come there are still so many vastly different methods of teaching literacy? Why do people still argue about it?

This book sets out to ask and answer these three crucial questions. I certainly don't know if there is a simple answer to any of them. They are as complex as many great philosophical questions. They are questions about society, behaviour, power, money, thought, knowledge, education, humanity and science.

The second section documents the history of this great debate, as well as major government-level inquiries that have delved into these questions.

During the research phase of this book, I made vigorous efforts to step outside my own comfort zone and gather information from sources I didn't necessarily agree with. What I noticed was that many of those sources had common characteristics despite the low quality of their offerings. One in particular was the extensive use of catchphrases. I say 'catchphrases' to emphasise that they are distinct from academic language. Catchphrases are associated with particular people and groups, whereas academic language is used across disciplines to describe testable, replicable phenomena. 'Barking at print' is a catchphrase and doesn't have a distinct definition, whereas 'hyperlexia' is academic language and can be precisely defined.

People who use catchphrases are difficult to argue with, since the imprecise terms they use can then be altered to 'move the goalposts' in discussions.

This reminded me of the way cults use language to simultaneously bind and isolate devotees. So I wrote a section about that. I included dyslexia in that section, as it is a condition that attracts all kinds of weird and wonderful 'remedies'. Dyslexia is also a bellwether for effective teaching. So often I see teachers displaying 'writing samples' to try and convince others of their effectiveness as teachers. Yet I only ever see the samples written by their top-performing students. My contention is that if you want to judge a teacher's effectiveness, you do so by the output and progress of their lowest performers.

The final section is written to provide some resources for teachers of those lowest performers. These are the students who, unless effectively taught from the first day of school, end up in private tuition if they can afford it and, all too often, the criminal justice system if they can't. They are consistently let down by schools that favour low quality methods of reading instruction.

We know what to do and we need to get on with it. At some point, I will write a book about schools that decided to adopt a no-fail attitude to teaching reading. But for now, this book is a starting point to help parents and teachers demand and supply a better deal for all children.

Free resources

Researching the topics outlined in this book became something akin to peering into fractals generated by the Mandelbrot Set. I've had to expunge thousands of words, just to keep it all manageable. Many of the words, resources and sections I have taken out are available on my website as blogs.

I have also recorded videos of many of the lessons described in the final chapters of the book as a free guide. They are available on my website, www. lifelongliteracy.com and through my Lyn Stone YouTube channel.

Acknowledgements

This book could not have existed without the help of my many colleagues, peers and those in the field who have contributed to the betterment of education for all.

It wasn't until I started the chapter on the major players that I began to get really attached to this project. Looking into the history of the great debate and putting faces to the names I'd seen over and over again in my reading on this subject, I began to feel like I was visiting old friends. To make sure I was doing them justice, I wrote to as many of the living candidates as I could, and tried to make sure I was representing their 'big ideas' and notable publications properly.

Many of them graciously answered my questions and steered me with kindness, openness and generosity. I felt like I wanted to do this particular project forever.

Here in Australia, certain living legends of academia need to be thanked for tolerating my dumb questions and letting my voice be heard. They are Jennifer Buckingham, Max Coltheart, Lorraine Hammond, Kerry Hempenstall, Molly de Lemos, Pamela Snow and Kevin Wheldall.

The strength, determination and wisdom of the dyslexia admins and activists here in Australia/New Zealand never fails to astound me. I know I have probably left someone out, but I thank you all, you formidable dissidents: Sarah Allen, Sarah Asome, Kate Bertoncello, Elise Cassidy, Vikki CH, Alison Clarke, Jen Cross, Belinda Dekker, Tanya Forbes, Heidi Gregory, Anita Evans Hellevik, Julie Hermansen, Leanne James, Liz Kane, Victoria Leslie, Sandra Marshall, Julie Mavlian, Carolyn Merritt, Susan Milner, Georgina Perry, Vicky Saville and Sandra Tidswell.

A special word for someone who has become a trusted friend and advisor: Sweet by name and nature, Bob Sweet has been an unexpected treasure. He kindly shouldered many of the major burdens of this project and without his advice, this book would be so much less.

Acknowledgements

The UK contingent must also be mentioned, Debbie Hepplewhite and Sir Jim Rose, to be specific. Your sagacity is matched only by your benevolence.

My terrific editing team need thanking. They are the pragmatic and flawless Chris Burdess and the incomparable linguistic genius Isabelle Duquennois. Thanks also to those who have looked at and commented on bits and pieces, all highly valued: Fiona Duffy, Catherine and Richard Riordan, Kenny Reay and Tina Zitzlaff.

Bruce Roberts, commissioning editor at Routledge, has been a source of great encouragement. I must also thank Routledge editorial assistant Alice Gray, for such promptness and precision during this process.

My wonderful family, as usual, have been supportive and resilient. I am very lucky to have you all. So many we grudged sair to the land o' the leal during this project. I would have given up had it not been for you.

Similarly to my friends, many of whom I have already mentioned, I say this: thank you for checking in on me. We will be fine.

Not least are my fabulous students. You are some of the strongest people I know and it's a pleasure to have worked with each and every one of you. The same goes for the teachers in my life, past and present; such a lot of dedication and good will.

You have all taught me unforgettable lessons.

With thanks to Aidan Potts for artwork for Figures 17.1, 17.2, 17.3, 17.4, 17.6, 17.7, 17.9, 18.1, 18.2, 18.4, 18.5 and to Ailsa Dunnachie-Young for Figures 16.1 and 24.1.

A simple view

Some stages of learning to read and write take longer, require more practice and demand better instruction than others. For example, learning whether text in your language goes from left to right or right to left is fairly easy, and once learned, is seldom forgotten.

Learning to convert the symbols on the page to speech is another matter. Language is a reflection of the workings of the mind and is therefore necessarily complex, even at the oral level. Adding writing to the picture puts an additional code-making/code-breaking component into an already complex structure.

Human writing systems have only been around for 3,000 years or so, and though they convey oral language, they did not develop in the same way as oral language. It's a good idea to remember this when thinking about how children are taught to read. Here are some basic principles that can help.

- Reading and writing is not the same as listening and speaking. Therefore, we get better results when we remove the expectation that children will just start reading in the same way as they just started speaking.
- *Learning* to read is not the same as *skilled* reading. Therefore, we get better results when we are aware of the process of learning to read and when we teach towards that. Skilled reading is a destination; the journey is somewhat different.

Falsehoods flourish in the presence of complexity, and, even to this day, there are people who not only believe, but viciously defend outdated, demonstrably incorrect views of reading. The two major false ideas can be classified as *whole language* and *whole word* approaches to teaching reading.

When poor reasoning occurs, the vulnerable inevitably suffer. In many cases, a lack of understanding of the building blocks of literacy leads to poor teaching and ineffective intervention (Figure 1.1).

Phonics	Whole language	Wholeword
• Teach the relationship between sounds and symbols.	• Immerse children in language and they will learn to read naturally.	• Teach children whole words, since they read whole words.

Figure 1.1 The three major theories of reading

The Simple View and dual coding

To begin with, any theory of reading instruction must have a perspective on what reading actually is.

Reading experts often refer to the Simple View of Reading (Gough & Tunmer 1986). This is a formula designed to help educators assess and assist readers.

The Simple View states that skill level in reading comprehension can be predicted by measuring two processes:

1. word recognition
2. language comprehension

So, the better you can convert the letters on the page into sounds and words, and the more words you understand, the more you'll be able to comprehend what you're reading (Figure 1.2).

The Simple View of Reading is a logical, testable formula grounded in decades of research.

Along with this, and slightly more technical, the Dual-Route Approach is a model of reading aloud which suggests that two separate cognitive pathways are involved in and available for the pronunciation of a written word (Coltheart 2007). Those pathways are the phonological and the semantic. The phonological route assists in reading all words, whilst the semantic route can only assist in reading regular or known real words.

Dual Route Theory is fascinating, but too complex for this book. Further reading is highly recommended, however. I mention it because it explains the confusion that educators sometimes experience when comparing the journey to the destination in reading.

The Big Six

Word-level recognition relies on six key skills. First referred to as The Big Five (Chall 1983), and later on – with the addition of oral language development – as the Big Six (Konza 2014), they are:

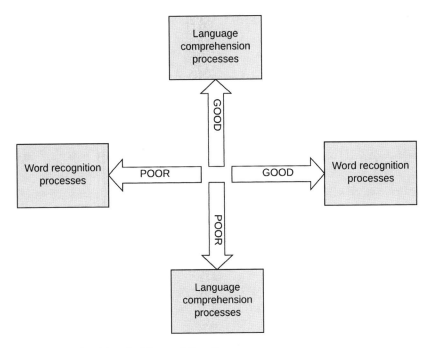

Figure 1.2 The Simple View of Reading

1. oral language development
2. phonological (including phonemic) awareness
3. phonics
4. fluency
5. vocabulary
6. comprehension

This section defines each skill. Later on, Section 4 builds on this information to provide a helpful guide to assessing and teaching these and related skills.

Many in opposition to, or who do not fully understand, the science of reading will lump all of the above under the umbrella of 'phonics'. A better description would perhaps be 'structured literacy'.

Whole language: A linguistic profile

There are other perspectives which fail to link decoding to comprehension, or which place undue emphasis on comprehension and dismiss decoding altogether.

Back in the 1960s, there was a movement in educational circles which claimed that a code-based, systematic approach to teaching reading was wrong. This general kind of challenge to convention, conformity and authority was popular and led to many great changes in civil rights, etc. In education, however, it led to the disastrous rise of whole language.

It is not easy to pin whole language down to one single definition. Whole language is more of a force, a set of ideas and a suite of related methodologies. It is based on two flawed principles:

1. That children learn to read in much the same way that they learn to talk (they don't), because learning to read is a natural process (it's not).
2. That immersing children in a literacy-rich environment will lead them to discover the structure of the written code by themselves (it won't).

There are few people who describe themselves as whole language practitioners or who say their methods are whole language based, but there are certain words and characteristics associated with the movement.

Firstly, anyone talking about 'making meaning' or 'meaning-making' is likely to be using resources from a whole language background. When referring to the process of reading, keywords like:

- sampling,
- noticing,
- reading behaviours,
- literacy events,
- authentic text,
- observation,
- word-solving,
- a range of strategies, and
- get your mouth ready

are also whole language red flags.

Next are the cute, but ultimately empty catchphrases that whole language proponents use to try and discredit structured literacy, especially systematic synthetic phonics:

- drill and kill
- talk and chalk
- reading is caught not taught
- barking at print
- all children learn differently
- no one size fits all

The most significant and endemic legacy of whole language is the *Three-Cueing System* (a.k.a. the *Searchlight Model*), methodologies based on the Reading Recovery program and the emerging *balanced literacy* movement.

In a disastrous misinterpretation of the underlying processes activated through reading, the Three-Cueing System has been developed, repeated and drummed into novice teachers since about 1986. It has *no* basis in science and runs counter to what we know about how words are lifted off the page (Adams 1998).

I am loath to give it oxygen, so in very brief summary, it is a (failed) model of the strategies children are supposed to use when reading words. It has developed into a system of coaching that downplays phonics, requires very little expertise and places the burden of learning to read on the child, the whole child and no one but the child.

Relying on oral language alone and using guessing – rather than decoding – is a dead end for many students. Cueing systems aside, whole language goes by several different names and has various guises, summarised below.

Guided reading

A small group approach where teachers attempt to use meaning and picture cues to get children to practise and read aloud a prescribed text. The text is usually selected based on the outdated and useless Running Records system of reading assessment, so even then, it is not appropriate reading material.

Pause, prompt, praise

Often used to try to guide parents listening to their children read, the *pause, prompt, praise* framework is just another way of trying to get children to connect to oral language without sounding out. The pause part is good, the prompt part is threadbare and the praise part is lovely but won't help them develop a love of reading like it's supposed to if they can't actually decode the words.

Literacy levels

There are many systems in schools that place children into reading groups and in reading levels. In fact, there are gigantic, lucrative systems of levelled readers and their whole language accompaniments everywhere.

Whole word: A cognitive load too far

The whole word method was also proven widely ineffective because, once again, its starting point was the assumption that because children speak in whole words, they should learn read in whole words too. This theory is alive and well today throughout primary education.

Whenever you see a list of words sent home on flashcards, in a book or on a worksheet for children to learn for a test, in the absence of any explicit instruction on *how* they might be learned, you are seeing whole word teaching in action.

Edward Dolch was one of the earlier whole word proponents. The strength of his and other whole word advocates' arguments lies in the fact that children do need to be able to instantly recognise and spell a certain number of high frequency words before they can become fluent readers and writers.

No one is disputing this. The problem, though, lies in the fact that instant, whole word recall does not come about through instant, whole word learning. A child can only rote-learn so much before the demands on memory become too great. It is much easier to teach children how to blend and segment words using an ever more sophisticated store of sound/symbol patterns.

Very few people can learn all the words in their language as individual units. The cognitive demands placed on a child when using this method are too high in most cases. It also doesn't give them any hope of reading unfamiliar words or spelling much at all.

Unlike whole language, there isn't as much of an army of whole word fanatics, trying to push political and educational agendas towards this method. That hasn't stopped the technique from seeping into classrooms the world over. Whole word flashcards, 'magic words' lists, word-shape worksheets and reading material with a heavy emphasis on repetition are symptoms of this approach and they are everywhere. Whole word and whole language often overlap, presenting a doubly damaging effect to anyone but the very fortunate.

Why don't we all teach structured literacy?

Whole language and whole word approaches offer two things that structured literacy doesn't, and this accounts somewhat for their widespread popularity:

1. Ease: Teachers do not have to have a great deal of expertise to use these approaches, since they are based on children 'discovering' how written language works for themselves.
2. Absolution: Children who make no or low progress in reading and writing are labelled within these approaches as having deficits beyond the teacher's control, such as a language disorder or a social disadvantage.

Structured literacy teaching requires expertise and practice, along with a depth and breadth of knowledge not usually required of graduate teachers.

Structured literacy, delivered effectively, equips teachers to teach reading and adequate writing to *all* their students. It is a no-fail approach.

As Louisa Moats (1999) says, 'Teaching reading *is* rocket science'.

References

Adams, M. J. (1998). The Three-Cueing System. In F. Lehr & J. Osborn (Eds.), *Literacy for All Issues in Teaching and Learning*, pp. 73–99. New York: Guilford Press.

Chall, J. S. (1983). *Stages of Reading Development*. New York: McGraw-Hill.

Coltheart, M. (2007). Modeling Reading: The Dual Route Approach. In *The Science of Reading: A Handbook*, pp. 6–23. Carlton, Victoria: Blackwell.

Gough, P. B., & Tunmer, W. E. (1986). Decoding, Reading, and Reading Disability. *Remedial and Special Education*, 7(1), 6–10. doi:10.1177/074193258600700104

Konza, D. (2014). Teaching Reading: Why the "Fab Five" Should Be the "Big Six". *Australian Journal of Teacher Education*, 39(12), 153–69.

Moats, L. (1999). *Teaching Reading Is Rocket Science*. Washington, DC: American Federation of Teachers.

CHAPTER 2

Oral language development

A belief that we can make a difference for children from poorly resourced families is a critical starting point.

John Hattie

No other creature can form and express thought with the depth and richness of a human. Through countless generations, wisdom and mythology have passed from mouth to ear. We are neurologically programmed to speak and listen.

We spend a great deal of our childhood learning to speak. The words we process and store during that time, especially pre-school, arrive mostly through oral language.

Of course, linguistic development doesn't just involve creating a store of known words. It also leads to greater understanding of shades of meaning, leading to social skills, such as the importance of saying *please* and *thank you*, the insight to know when someone is joking, and the ability to take turns when listening and speaking.

The quality of a child's oral language at the point of school entry is largely dependent on how much they are spoken to and read to from birth. A famous study in the 1990s showed differences of up to 30 million exposures to words before entering school in a group of children. This oral advantage showed up in vocabulary, language and comprehension skills when tested years later (Hart & Risley 1995).

This clear gap in oral language, which widens in the absence of high quality instruction, is known as the Matthew Effect. The name refers to the Bible passage in Matthew stating something to the effect of the rich getting richer and the poor getting poorer (Stanovich 1986).

Oral language deficits are best addressed by speech-language pathologists if an underlying disorder is suspected. However, good initial teaching in a mainstream setting can be sufficient for the majority of students entering school despite their background.

Though much oral language development begins in the pre-school period, school is the bridge between oral language and the more formal, structured language known as *literate language*.

Literate language includes

- summarising
- talking about the past and future
- explaining how things work
- storytelling
- figurative language

Oral language continues to develop in range and complexity throughout a child's schooling. At any stage of the reading process, oral language is the foundation. This is well illustrated in the Simple View of Reading (see Chapter 1).

The Simple View formulates two basic components to reading: decoding (using the alphabetic code, and later, word recognition from memory, to identify words) and linguistic comprehension (knowing what individual and combinations of words mean).

Children with rich oral language and no underlying developmental language disorder tend to pick up reading more quickly and with less teaching. If you go back to the Simple View, this stands to reason, since children who understand more words are likely to be able to connect to the meaning of the words they are reading.

Whether a child's environment is language-rich or not, literacy is still achievable with skilled instruction. A child with lower oral language may make a teacher's job harder, but it also makes a teacher's job more important.

The least effective type of reading instruction is any method that fails to untangle linguistic comprehension and decoding.

Oral language development and learning to read are not identical processes. Whole language theory draws parallels with the driving force behind a child learning their native language and a child learning to read and write. That is, their success comes from a desire to understand and be understood. This is where the phrase 'meaning-making' comes from.

In support of this theory, whole language proponents will argue that children don't learn the individual sounds of their language when they are learning to talk, so why should they when they are learning to read? Instead, they establish their skills through trial and error, observation and word-level cues like context and pictures.

This may be all very well for a certain percentage of the population who manage to intuit individual sounds and symbols without explicit instruction, but it consigns an unacceptably large portion to the wastelands of illiteracy. It is a distortion of the role of oral language and is dangerous in two ways:

1. Low oral language ability is often used as an excuse by whole language proponents when they fail to successfully teach those in need of explicit, code-based instruction.
2. High oral language ability masks the performance of many children who struggle with decoding and encoding. These children can become expert guessers and look as if they are progressing, and that whole language interventions are working, but this is a temporary glow.

Research has shown that children's oral language development does indeed tune them in to the sound structure of the language, supporting their emerging understanding of the fact that speech can be turned into print and that print can be turned into speech (Dickinson et al. 2003; Goswami 2001; Whitehurst & Lonigan 1998). This is known as the *alphabetic principle*.

Further still, there is a population within all socioeconomic groups who will not pick up reading and/or writing very well at all, unless properly identified and expertly taught. This condition is described with several labels, the most common of all being *dyslexia*. We will return to this term later.

Many children with dyslexia have very strong oral language and high linguistic comprehension. What they lack is skill and experience in decoding and encoding.

Teaching them to draw on their oral language and to avoid decoding robs them of crucial practice. They may even experience success at first, because of their strong oral language, but as the demands and volume of text increase, they have nothing to fall back on and ultimately make slow or no progress.

Why early intervention is important

When the focus on learning to read shifts to a focus on reading to learn, children who have not mastered the written code begin to suffer from what some call the 'Fourth Grade Slump' (Chall & Jacobs 2003).

Children from diverse backgrounds come to see me in my practice. They all struggle with reading and writing. Due to the advocacy of grass-roots groups working hard to raise awareness of developmental disorders, this population has been getting younger and younger. Parents are becoming more likely to trust their instincts and ignore any 'wait and see' comments that can sometimes be made at school.

This wasn't always the case. The majority of students I used to see were boys in the third and fourth year of school. They were often very skilled listeners and speakers, with large, robust vocabularies. Most of them had managed to fake their reading progress by falling back on their oral language. More often than not, unsuitable tools were used to assess their reading, such as Running Records and predictable texts. The wrong components of reading were blamed for their lack of progress, and so they didn't raise any alarms until complexity began to set in.

Their spelling was also usually very poor, but overall, their low progress was accepted and parents were told that they would somehow catch up as they matured. Without intervention, many children in this situation simply never do.

The scene is changing. Nowadays, many of my students are in their first or second year of school, and I am thankful for that. They are much easier to help for two main reasons:

1. They have not strongly developed the regrettable habit of guessing, which has to be carefully undone and replaced with more effective strategies.
2. They have not yet turned away from reading and writing as excruciating, stressful activities.

Dyslexic or not, children who enter school with diminished oral language and/or make slow progress in learning to read need to be noticed and supported.

References

Chall, J. S., & Jacobs, V. A. (2003). Poor Children's Fourth-Grade Slump. *American Educator*, 27(Spring), 14–15.

Dickinson, D. K., McCabe, A., Anastasopoulos, L., Peisner-Feinberg, E. S., & Poe, M. D. (2003). The Comprehensive Language Approach to Early Literacy: The Interrelationships Among Vocabulary, Phonological Sensitivity, and Print Knowledge Among Preschool-Aged Children. *Journal of Educational Psychology*, 95(3), 465–81.

Goswami, U. (2001). Early Phonological Development and the Acquisition of Literacy. In S. B. Neuman & D. K. Dickinson (Eds.), *Handbook of Early Literacy Research*, pp. 111–25. New York: Guilford Press.

Hart, B., & Risley, T. R. (1995). *Meaningful Differences in the Everyday Experience of Young American Children*. Baltimore: Paul H. Brookes.

Hattie, J. (2015). *What Doesn't Work in Education: The Politics of Distraction*. London: Pearson.

Stanovich, K. E. (1986). Matthew Effects in Reading: Some Consequences of Individual Differences in the Acquisition of Literacy. *Reading Research Quarterly*, 21(4), 360–407.

Whitehurst, G. J., & Lonigan, C. J. (1998). Child Development and Emergent Literacy. *Child Development*, 69(3), 848–72.

CHAPTER 3

Phonological awareness

Broadly speaking, phonological awareness (PA) is a sensitivity to the sounds and sound patterns of language (Figure 3.1). PA can be measured and can help form accurate predictions about reading ability.

PA is the ability to perceive and manipulate the following word parts:

- syllables
- onsets
- rimes
- phonemes

Let's look at each one.

Syllables (syl-la-bles)

Origin: Greek *syn* 'together' + *lemma* 'something taken'. Interestingly, the Latin origin of *comprehend* also means to take together (*com + praehendere*).

A syllable is a word or part of a word that can be made with one impulse of the voice. Syllables are beats, clusters of sounds with vowels as their nucleus and consonants gathered around them.

There are many approaches to counting syllables in words and being able to identify them is useful in reading and spelling. Syllables are easier to perceive than the separate sounds (phonemes) they contain.

Every syllable in every word has one vowel sound. For example, the word *button* has two vowel letters and two syllables. We have a 1:1 match between vowel letters and syllables. This is typical of English words, which is why counting and identifying syllables is a reliable way of learning to read and write longer words.

As with most aspects of language, there are complications. Being comfortable with and able to explain the complexities of certain syllables is an advantage for teachers.

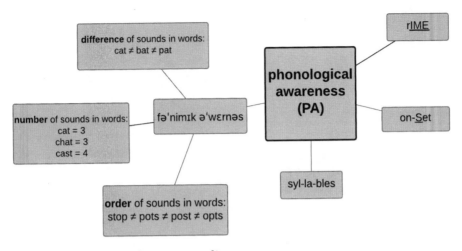

Figure 3.1 Phonological awareness diagram

There are some literacy programs which name and practise different 'syllable types'. These can usually be found amongst what is collectively known as the Orton-Gillingham (OG) suite of resources. These types offer a fascinating insight into the structure of words.

Onsets (on-Sets)

An onset is a part of a syllable that precedes the vowel or vowel sound. The /p/ in *pat*, the /b/ in *big* and the /s/ and /p/ in *spin* are all onsets.

Not all syllables have an onset. Take the word *onset*, for example. The first syllable begins with a vowel. There is no onset in the first syllable. The second syllable does have an onset; it is the letter <s>.

In English, we don't have onsets containing more than three consonants (*string*, *splash*, *scream*). And we're lucky. Some languages only allow two, if that. All languages have rules regarding consonant clusters in the onset position. These rules are called *phonotactic constraints.*

Polish is quite liberal with its consonant clusters. It allows up to four consonants in the onset position, e.g. *pstrag* ('trout') and five at the end of words, e.g. *pierogisktrz* (like pierogi, Polish dumplings, but apparently more delicious!).

It stands to reason that clusters of consonants are constrained in language. Too many together are difficult to perceive, pronounce and spell. People who struggle with PA often have problems perceiving embedded consonants, especially in the onset position. For example, the word *slip*, which has a two-consonant onset (the letters <s> and <l>), might be read or spelled 'sip' by a person struggling with PA.

Many schools teach onsets as whole units and call them 'blends'. Children often come into my practice and tell me that there are three sounds in the word *slip*: /sl/ + /ɪ/ + /p/. This is fairly innocuous on the surface, but when it comes to spelling, low-progress readers will then fail to notice the embedded <l> and spell *slip* 'sip'. It happens constantly and is the reason why PA assessment and remediation is essential for anyone who struggles.

Having said that, intensive PA training for typically developing readers has been the subject of academic debate for many years and still has various conclusions. In good, systematic, synthetic phonics programs, PA emerges for most children without direct, intensive PA training. There are some children who do need a booster in their PA and teachers do benefit from knowing what that is.

Rimes (rIMES)

The rime is the part of the syllable containing the vowel sound and any consonants afterwards. You can further divide a rime into a nucleus (the vowel part) and a coda (literally, the tail). The rime is what makes words rhyme.

Yes, the words *rhyme* and *rime* are confusingly similar. Both can be traced back to the Greek word for *rhythm*.

For many children, rime sensitivity begins in the pre-school stage. Nursery rhymes, songs and poems form an instinctive part of parental/caregiver communication with babies and infants. This is another reason that children who are talked to and read to have a much better chance at acquiring reading than those who come from less advantaged homes.

Talking and reading to children is important for setting up strong structures for reading, but please bear in mind, it doesn't *teach* reading and it certainly doesn't teach writing.

Phonemic awareness /fəˈnimɪk əˈwɛrnəs/[1]

A very important subset of PA is phonemic awareness. The two terms get used interchangeably sometimes, but they are distinct from one another. PA is knowledge of many different aspects of speech sounds, whereas phonemic awareness solely addresses the smallest units of sound (phonemes).

Phonemic awareness is the ability to perceive and manipulate individual sounds within words.

When reading and writing, the requirements of memory and processing speed are high, and in the case of low PA, perceiving, ordering, numbering and differentiating sounds in words can be tough and thankless.

One final note about PA, just to help avoid confusion and to address the arguments of those who may dismiss PA as an important component of literacy:

There is a myth making its rounds in educational circles that PA has little or no impact on reading after the second year of school. This is actually a misrepresentation of the facts.

As children mature, vocabulary knowledge and low processing speed become more reliable as predictors of reading ability.

Similarly, if a child at the age of five knows the first letter of their name, you might predict that they will be better at reading than a child at five who doesn't. By the time children reach the age of eight or nine, very few of them don't know the first letter of their name, so that test begins to lack validity.

Therefore, it is unwise to dismiss PA, even if it can be higher in older children who are poor readers. PA is critical to all.

The good news is that PA can be measured, directly taught and practised to levels which allow progress in literacy. In fact, any high quality beginning reading programs will have PA measuring and mastery components written into them.

Note

1 The phonetic transcription of the words *phonemic awareness* relates to my accent, which is Scottish and therefore *rhotic* (we pronounce <r> after vowels).

Phonics

Once upon a time there were three different theories of reading instruction:

1. Phonics
2. Whole word
3. Whole language

These competing theories have led to what is known as the *Reading Wars* or sometimes the *great debate*.

Scientific consensus indicates that phonics is more efficient, economical and more widely beneficial as an initial instructional method than the other two. I could fill the rest of this book with references to support that statement; not so in support of whole word or whole language. In his seminal work *Language at the Speed of Sight*, Mark Seidenberg sums it up perfectly:

> *Learning to read is more difficult when the development of phonemic representations is impaired or discouraged by educational practices.*

(28)

Teaching the 26 symbols of English and their relationship to the 44 (or so) speech sounds is called phonics. Low phonological awareness (PA) is a barrier to early literacy, but can be skilfully addressed through phonics. Teaching whole words or contextual guessing does very little, if nothing, to increase PA.

Not all phonics methods are created equal, though. To complicate matters further, there are three main approaches to teaching phonics:

*   synthetic phonics
*   analytic phonics
*   embedded phonics (now emerging within the 'balanced literacy' approach)

There is also a method closely related to synthetic phonics called *linguistic phonics*. Both methods systematically and explicitly teach phoneme–grapheme correspondences, but linguistic phonics does so always within the context of a word, whereas synthetic phonics teaches graphemes and their common sounds inside and outside words. I find the debate between proponents of the two tedious, but if I had to come down in favour of one over the other, synthetic phonics would win, because of its wide application to the largest population of children.

Here is the difference between the three methods, illustrated with Wingdings.

Synthetic phonics

Synthetic derives from a Greek word meaning 'place together'. It does not mean, in this case, artificial or unnatural. This is a badly thoughtout straw man argument against phonics. When you hear it, you know the depth and breadth of the speaker's understanding of the process. Point, laugh if you must, and then ignore.

Synthetic in this instance means a building, a *synthesis* of elements. Synthetic phonics goes from parts to whole. The parts are the small units of sound (phonemes) in words, represented by combinations of alphabetic letters.

In synthetic phonics, beginning readers are shown a series of symbols and are taught the first and most common sound that goes along with them. Later on, they are shown how to put the symbols together to create words. Later still, if this type of synthetic phonics is systematic, all of the alphabet letters and sounds and many of the combinations are introduced and practised.

Students are also shown how to segment words back into their individual sounds, thus providing a framework for spelling too.

How it works

Your teacher has been showing you these symbols all week and has been making their sounds at the same time. You've been repeating the sounds and practising writing the symbols (fortunately, English letter symbols are much easier to write than Wingdings):

♦ = /s/
♋ = /æ/
□ = /p/
◆ = /t/
⌖ = /ɪ/
■ = /n/

If the pace is really good, your teacher might even show you how to blend these symbols when they appear in groups and get you to practise them, from left to right, saying the whole word afterwards. Soon, you'll be able to read the words below, and you'll be able to sound out other words that your teacher hasn't even shown you:

♦♋♦

⬜✠■

♦♋⬜

♋♦

♋■♦

As with Wingdings, there is one symbol, or combination of symbols, for every sound in the language. You will learn and practise all of this in a systematic, logical order, going from simple to complex.

With lots of practice and guidance, you and just about everyone else in your class will be reading and writing an ever-increasing range of words.

Don't get me wrong. That's not all there is to reading, but it's a strong foundation. If taught systematically, it provides the means to lift the vast majority of children towards literacy, regardless of their background, their PA or their oral language development.

Analytic phonics

You are shown whole words and asked to notice similarities between the words. Sometimes the words even have a picture beside them to help you figure out what the word is. Here is an analytic phonics set, for example:

mat, make, man, moo

You are directed to analyse the word and observe that the first letter is the same in all the words, therefore that symbol must represent /m/.

Your teacher puts a list of words on the board and reads them to you.

⊙♋♦⬚ ⊙♋&ⅿ⬚ ⊙♋■ ⊙⬜⬜

The teacher reads the word to you and then gets you to notice the first letter in each. You notice they are the same. You practise writing this symbol and you say the sound for it.

Then you get a worksheet with some pictures of various objects and you have to put a circle round the ones that start with ⊙.

This goes on for a while and then you're introduced to a new set of words that begin with a different symbol.

This goes on for about a year. You flutter around whole words in the hope that you can make the connection.

Sometimes there will be a chart on the wall and/or a chart on your desk with boxes containing a picture to make you think of a sound, and all the different Wingdings that can make that sound. You are supposed to memorise all this and apply it to new words when you read and write.

Some of you will have picked up that the symbols represent sounds and will have even figured out the sound–symbol relationship in symbols you haven't been taught yet. This is called implicit learning and has a significant role in education of any kind. However, the majority of beginners need explicit teaching as a baseline for further learning.

Some of you, though, will not have made strong enough connections and, by the end of the year, will not be able to read or spell much at all.

Some of you will have difficulty remembering, accessing, stringing together, recognising, pronouncing and/or writing the symbols and by the end of the *third* year, will still not be able to read or spell much at all.

Embedded phonics

There is a type of phonics that I call *fake phonics* or *alt-phonics,* but it sometimes goes by the name of embedded, incidental or implicit phonics. To give the impression of 'balanced literacy', some teachers will include a nod to phonics in the context of actual literature. They place great emphasis on 'authentic text' whilst ignoring authentic research.

Just to clarify: I am a huge fan of good literature for children. However, if children get systematic, explicit instruction as well as controlled, decodable texts at the beginning of their journey into literacy, they fare better. Many systematic phonics programs rightly supply such texts. There is nothing wrong with this kind of scaffolding.

How it works

You are given a book with lots of great pictures and not much text. The teacher tells you it's all about dogs and the places they go. You talk about some of the places you think dogs might go. Figure 4.1 provides an example of a picture and its accompanying text:

Figure 4.1 ❄︎≈︎♏︎ ♎︎□︎❑︎ ⍓︎♦ ⍓︎■ ◆︎≈︎♏︎ ♐︎♏︎♎︎ 🖂

The teacher asks you what you see and you say you see a dog in a car. Your teacher reads the sentence and you are asked to point to the words and repeat the sentence. You listen as the teacher says, 'The dog is in the car.' You repeat the sentence and point to the words.

Good job! You are reading! Ready for the next page? What do you think you might see on the next page?

If you make a mistake, your teacher will tell you to look at the picture, and if that doesn't help, your teacher will ask you what makes sense in the sentence. If you guess right often enough, you'll be allowed to move onwards and upwards.

If you guess wrong, your teacher might point to the first letter and ask/tell you what the first sound is. If you can guess the word from that, great! If you

Figure 4.2 ❄︎≈︎♏︎ ♎︎□︎❑︎ ⍓︎♦ ⍓︎■ ◆︎≈︎♏︎ ♍︎□︎□︎ 🖂

can't, the teacher will tell you the word and move on. That's the phonics part. The first letter. That's it.

You'll get lots of books like this sent home and your parents will be told to use meaning or sentence structure cues to correct you.

Some of you may have started to figure out the code. Six months of this and many of you will have memorised the pattern for some of our common words. Many of you will not and some of you never will using this method. That's because it doesn't work very well at all.

Whilst working on a draft of this section, one of my daughters came and sat next to me and asked me what I was doing. I explained that I was writing about the illusion of reading and showed her the dog pictures with the Wingdings. She pointed to each 'word' and read it all beautifully. Now *that's* barking at print!

Even synthetic phonics has variation

To be as effective as possible for as many students as possible, a synthetic phonics program has to have certain qualities. Synthetic phonics has to be:

a. Explicit

This means that the teacher carefully explains the relationships between the sounds and symbols, paces those explanations well and checks for understanding. It doesn't mean that the teacher does all the talking, but it does mean that explanations are thorough enough for children to start being independent readers and writers.

One common mistake is to confuse pacing with explicitness. Some teachers will introduce a new sound or symbol at the rate of one or two per week. This is not fast enough. The children who are advanced will become bored and disengaged and the children who need the most help will not have the opportunity to use this knowledge with enough variety to continue succeeding.

b. Systematic

Good teaching in any subject has at its core the correct balance of *scope* and *sequence*. This is systematic teaching.

Scope means the depth and breadth that is appropriate for the situation. A beginning reader might not benefit from being taught that the symbols <ough> can represent six different sounds. Instead, they would benefit straight away from learning the basic consonant and vowel sounds of the alphabet.

Sequence refers to the order in which the symbols and sounds are taught. We have the order of the alphabet, and this is fine, but a common sequence is something like <s,a,p,t,i,n> – which follows an order of commonality in the first 200 or so words in most elementary word lists.

Systematic synthetic phonics (SSP) programs do differ in this sequence, which is an interesting point. You might wonder why there isn't a prescribed order for all phonics programs.

In trying to figure out the answer, I made a chart of eight systematic synthetic phonics programs and compared the order of the first ten symbols (see Figure 4.3). They are quite different.

Spalding introduces the 26 letters of the alphabet according to their formation, since writing is an integral part of the Spalding program. This makes sense.

Lindamood LiPS introduces the symbols and sounds based on articulation, starting with the plosives at the front of the mouth and working back and introducing three vowel sounds and symbols to represent the smiley, open and round vowel extremes in English. This also makes sense.

Others stay close to the s-a-p-t-i-n pattern. Still others use a version of the *Carnine Sequence*, originated by educational psychologist Doug Carnine. The Carnine Sequence recommends:

- Letters and sounds should be dissimilar when introduced together, e.g. /d/ and /t/ should not be introduced together as they sound similar. Letters which look similar are also not introduced together, e.g. <m> and <n>.
- Sounds which can be lengthened or held on to are introduced early to facilitate blending, e.g. /m/ as opposed to /k/.

Program	1	2	3	4	5	6	7	8	9	10
Spalding	a	c	d	f	g	o	s	qu	b	e
Lindamood LiPS	p	b	t	d	k	g	ee	oo	u	f
Jolly Phonics	s	a	t	i	p	n	ck	e	h	r
Minilit	m	s	t	a	p	i	f	r	o	c
Little Learners Love Literacy	m	s	f	a	p	t	c	i	b	h
Teach your Child to Read in 100 Easy Lessons	m	s	a	e	t	r	ee	d	i	th
Phonics International	s	a	t	i	p	n	c	k	-ck	e
Read Write Inc.	m	a	s	d	t	i	n	p	g	o

Figure 4.3 The first ten symbols introduced in eight different phonics programs

- Common letters are introduced early so that a wide range of words can be generated.
- Lower case letters are introduced before upper case.

The Carnine Sequence in full:

a m t s i f d r o g l h u c b n k v e w j p y T L M F D I N A R H G B x q z J E Q

Each sequence has its own rationale and this is allowable for the following reason: There is no control over what beginning readers have had prior exposure to. All of them have different experiences of the different symbols in the alphabet. After all, the first thing a child usually learns to read and spell is his or her name. From Aaliah to Zander, and everything in between, this is a widely varied experience. So too are the books or words that a child has seen prior to school. There is no possible way to know that and to teach sound–symbol correspondences according to that.

What matters is that there is a system and that the system allows for practice and mastery at an appropriate pace.

c. Cumulative

Good explanations and a logical scope and sequence strengthen phonics programs, but excellent phonics teaching also builds on what has been previously taught. This is called cumulative instruction.

Like a rain cloud gathering water particles, cumulative instruction builds and extends from the known to the unknown in small, secure steps.

d. Diagnostic

The most efficient methods include a range of checks along the way to make sure all students are keeping up and progressing. They answer the following questions:

- Are you keeping up?
- If not, why not?
- What can be done to help you keep up?

The second two questions are more complex and require a high level of teacher knowledge and expertise.

The United Kingdom has introduced a Year One Phonics Check which provides answers to the first question. Moves are being made to introduce a similar check in Australia (in the face of bitter and baffling opposition).

Decodable vs. predictable readers

Initially, many synthetic phonics programs use books containing controlled texts, with words containing patterns recently introduced for extra practice. These are called 'decodable readers' and are a temporary scaffold to help children weave the strands of reading together. Please don't be fooled by anti-phonics statements saying that these texts kill the 'joy of reading'. They do nothing of the sort. They are intended as a bridge and they fade out when children's competence allows.

Not so for another type of beginning reading book called 'predictable readers'. These are books written specifically to encourage guessing from pictures or context. Sometimes they come in 'levelled' sets, where one book is deemed harder than another based on an arbitrary algorithm. Children are given comprehension-based tests to figure out their 'level' and then consigned to these predictable readers and levels for the rest of their early years.

Despite what your school might say, these are the books that kill the love of reading. Here is a line from a predictable reader intended for foundation children:

'Noah played with the dinosaur in the pool.'

Can you guess what the picture might be? This is in the absence of teaching any of the complex code needed to read or spell those words in a different context.

If you want to make a difference in your school, demand decodable readers and campaign to have levelled reading systems and predictable readers eradicated.

The biggest phonics fallacy

A classic straw man argument of those who oppose phonics is the assertion that there are some people who wish to teach literacy through phonics and phonics alone.

I'm not saying they don't exist, I'm just saying that they don't represent the established consensus among reading scientists.

What may have been a factor in this fallacy is the phrase 'first, fast and only'. This is about the use of phonics in early literacy acquisition and came about around the time of the Rose Report in the UK (see Chapter 12).

The word 'only' in this context refers to the strategy of sounding out words. 'Only' means not developing a reliance on picture cues, meaning cues or sentence structure cues. 'Only' ensures adequate early practice in sequencing and mapping the sounds of our language and the letters representing those sounds. 'Only' does not mean that phonics is the *only* part of the reading process.

Reference

Seidenberg, M. (2017). *Language at the Speed of Sight*. New York: Basic Books.

CHAPTER 5

Fluency

From Latin *flu-*, meaning *flowing*. We also get *fluid*, *flux* and *influenza* from this root.

Phonological awareness and phonics are teachable elements that require a systematic, diagnostic approach. These two elements contribute strongly to the third pillar of literacy: fluency. We will look at reading fluency first and then discuss fluent writing.

Reading fluency is a measure of three things:

**ACCURACY IN WORD DECODING X AUTOMATIC PROCESSING X
   PROSODIC READING**

Let's look at each element.

Accuracy in word decoding

A child with the ability to match symbols on the page to spoken sounds is already set up for a high degree of accuracy in word decoding. A child with a poor store of sound–symbol relationships will have less success.

There are several reasons why a child is inaccurate in word decoding:

- They have a developmental disorder such as dyslexia.
- They have not been explicitly taught the alphabetic code.
- They have been encouraged to guess at words using pictures, prediction, sentence structure or whole words.
- They suffer from a combination of all three above.

The fastest, most efficient, most generalisable way of increasing accuracy in word decoding is to make sure phonological awareness is sufficient and that the child has a strong foundation in systematic synthetic phonics.

Automatic processing: Practice, persistence and patience

Sounding words out is a terrific start, but at some point, all students have to make the leap from sounding to automatic processing. Three protective factors will help children make that leap.

The first is practice. I see my students for an hour a week. That's 1/168th of their lives. My job is to give them things to practise; not to be the only source of practice in their world. I tell parents that the real progress is made in the time that they don't see me. They *have* to practise.

Modelling good, fluent reading, of course, precedes this. No one on any side of the debate disagrees. For actual fluency practice, students need to be given daily opportunities to decode words, put them together in sentences and practise saying those sentences with confidence. Some will use their memory after the first few attempts, others will keep their eyes on the page. All of this is okay, but they need to practise.

Next is persistence. Reading doesn't come easy for some children, even when given the best early teaching. In less nurturing environments, children turn away from reading and writing altogether. In its most extreme form, a lack of persistence leads to *learned helplessness*, where they simply stop trying.

Getting students to persist is an art in itself. I run my lessons using a strict bribery and corruption policy. Everything we do is worth points, which in turn earn stickers, which in turn earn prizes. I don't care who says intrinsic motivation is its own reward. My students have often lost the will to persist and since I spend a lot of time asking them to persist at something that comes with a ton of emotional baggage, I have no qualms about offering incentives.

This is where feedback is vitally important. Giving children a roadmap by providing structured, systematic teaching with visible goals is helpful. By this, I do not mean the arbitrary levelled reading systems that seem to saturate primary schools. By feedback and roadmap, I refer to making sure children know that there is an alphabetic code, which will be learned over time, and showing them where they are on that progression towards automaticity.

Finally, there is patience. People do not get good at reading and writing overnight. People also have their own personal timeline. It is so tempting to shortcut reading development with temporary crutches like picture cues and semantic predictions. Children with strong oral language but poor phonological awareness will feel quite successful if allowed to circumvent the phonological route. Patience is required if we as parents and teachers are going to give all children the best deal.

As an adult, your ability to automatically process words is very high. You have a store of words that you can recognise instantly. In fact, it's very hard to turn off automatic processing once it's on. That's what makes the *Stroop Effect* so amusing.

The Stroop Effect, named after psychologist John Ridley Stroop, who did experiments on automaticity back in 1935, has seen something of a popularity spike online in the last decade. If you've seen those lists of colour words in different colour fonts, you'll know what the Stroop Effect is.

Try to say only the colour of the font in each word in Figure 5.1. You'll find that you have to hesitate and stop yourself from saying the actual word, whether you like it or not. This is because you automatically process words faster than you process names for colours.

The store of words a person can automatically process is often called the *sight word vocabulary.*

The whole-word method of teaching reading is built entirely on the flawed principle that multiple exposures to whole words are sufficient to teach reading. There is some truth to this argument for some people, and that seems good enough for many educators. I myself learned to start reading and spelling through this method. Maybe you did too. But that's because we had the sort of brain that happens to be optimum for that. We are the exception, not the rule.

A larger percentage of children learn to automatically process words if they are taught to break words apart and put words together through the systematic teaching of the alphabetic code. Increase in automatic processing is established by building strong phonic decoding skills first and allowing regular practice of text containing high frequency, decodable words.

Automatic processing is harder to establish by showing whole words and expecting children to simply memorise them by their shape or through other non-phonetic pathways. It's very tempting to be fooled into thinking a child can read when they use whole word memorisation. Sometimes this method can get them through the early years of primary school, but once the volume and complexity of text increases, the cognitive load is too great and those who haven't intuited the alphabetic code fall by the wayside. Still many schools send home lists of 'sight words' to be memorised from the first week of school because of the false, temporary impression of competence whole word memorisation creates. I have even been stunned to see spelling worksheets sent home with students with exercises such as those shown in Figure 5.2.

YELLOW BLUE ORANGE

Figure 5.1 The Stroop Effect

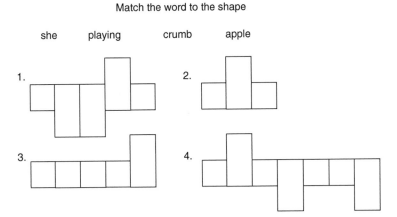

Figure 5.2 Word shapes worksheet

Need I elaborate? This is *not* what reading scientists mean when they refer to *patterns*. If you are using this technique, *please stop*. You are not teaching anything useful to any child, whether they are your top spellers or your struggling spellers. There is not one single study in the entire history of this planet which shows *any* benefit from doing this. It is mindless busy-work and it detracts from the real business of learning to read and write.

Patience pays. If we set children up with the tools to process the smallest units of written language, i.e. graphemes, they can then succeed at processing unknown words containing similar patterns. This takes longer, requires more knowledge on our part as teachers, and at first, is not nearly as impressive as the illusion of fluency that a small store of whole words can produce.

But if you want them to learn to spell these and similar words, you have to teach them the parts. This way, you help them with *orthographic mapping*. More on this shortly.

Prosodic reading

From Latin *pros* 'towards' + *oide* 'song'. It refers to a reader's ability to modulate their voice and use appropriate expression when reading aloud. 'Towards the song'. Isn't that nice?

Children who can decode efficiently generally have good prosody (Schwanenflugel, Hamilton, Wisenbaker, Kuhn & Stahl 2004). Decoding ability precedes prosody, so deciding where to focus instruction time depends on how well children can decode. With my students, we have a small portion of the lesson devoted to their 'performance piece', which is a set passage that they practise for prosody once it has been thoroughly decoded and under-stood. More about this in the Teaching Fluency chapter.

Reference

Schwanenflugel, P. J., Hamilton, A. M., Wisenbaker, J. M., Kuhn, M. R., & Stahl, S. A. (2004). Becoming a Fluent Reader: Reading Skill and Prosodic Features in the Oral Reading of Young Readers. *Journal of Educational Psychology*, 96(1), 119–29. http://doi.org/10.1037/0022-0663.96.1.119

CHAPTER 6

Vocabulary

From Latin *vocabularium*, 'a list of words', from the root *vox*, meaning 'voice'. We also get *vocal*, *vocation* and *evocative* from this root.

There are two branches of vocabulary that are distinct from one another, but which also overlap:

1. Sight word vocabulary: the store of words that are instantly recognisable to a reader, i.e. all the words you can read automatically.
2. Lexical-semantic vocabulary: the store of word meanings that readers or listeners can immediately access upon reading or hearing them, i.e. all the words and word-parts (prefixes, suffixes, etc.) that you can understand.

Though reading scientists don't always agree on the number of words and word-parts in a typical lexical-semantic vocabulary, it still fills one with a sense of wonder to realise how extensive a vocabulary can be. Stanislas Dehaene puts it beautifully in *Reading in the Brain*:

> *Any reader easily retrieves a single meaning out of at least 50,000 candidate words, in the space of a few tenths of a second, based on nothing more than a few strokes of light on the retina.*

Vocabulary itself can be further classified into tiers based on how often words are used in oral language, written language and domain-specific language (Beck, McKeowen & Kucan 2002). Figure 6.1 illustrates these tiers.

This framework helps teachers think about what to teach and how to teach it. Tier 1 contains words already in children's typical spoken vocabulary. Tier 2 contains words that can be added to children's vocabulary through explicit teaching; Tier 2 words can be taught if the underlying concepts are already known and if they can be explained simply. Tier 3 words contain words that are specific to precise domains, such as literature, science or law.

Tier	Description	Examples
Tier 1	Everyday words that require little or no instruction	ball, talk, funny, across
Tier 2	Words found in literature and written language, not generally picked up from everyday conversation	sphere, converse, droll, diagonally
Tier 3	Words that appear in specific domains	spheroid, discourse, meiotic, transversely

Figure 6.1 Vocabulary tiers

Does reading improve vocabulary?

When phonological awareness and phonics are established, slow progress in reading can continue to exist due to deficits in vocabulary. This loops back to oral language development.

Reading has important reciprocal effects for vocabulary. Vocabulary is built through reading, and reading proficiency increases through vocabulary knowledge. Figurative language, such as metaphor, simile, hyperbole and personification is not usually present in everyday speech. We turn to literature for this type of Tier 2 language.

This point is agreed upon by reading scientists and practitioners on all sides of the reading debate. What many fail to notice, however, is that you cannot assert that reading *builds* vocabulary and then postulate that children should learn to read by guessing.

Certain reading theorists claim that skilled readers make little or no use of phonic information, but prefer to guess words from context and sentence structure (Smith 1971). The opposite has been shown to be true, i.e. good readers pay attention to letters and poor readers are far more reliant on guessing (Stanovich 1980).

The same theorists also often state that reading leads to increased vocabulary. However, the proposition that good readers guess and that people build vocabulary through reading cannot be simultaneously true. Let's break it down.

IF good readers guess what the words are on the page with increasing efficiency ...

THEN they can only read words they already know ...

THEREFORE they can only add words to their vocabulary by *hearing* them. Not *reading* them.

THEREFORE reading cannot possibly increase vocabulary.

If you encourage guessing, there's no point in encouraging reading for vocabulary building. You choose.

Word families

It would be impossible to teach the definition of every single word in English, but that doesn't mean we can't teach children to be *generative*. Knowing how words work and having an understanding of a core of prefixes, roots and suffixes helps children generate the meaning of new words.

This then comes down to teacher knowledge and skill, and a willingness to never let a vocabulary-building opportunity go by. Unfortunately, the reality is often the opposite.

Take, for instance, the list of 'spelling words' my 11-year-old daughter brought home from school at the time of writing. She was in her last year of primary school and was fortunate enough to find herself in the 'advanced' spelling group.

She was given a list of unrelated words to memorise for a test every week. Only this year had she been asked to look them up in a dictionary and write their meanings. Her answers were seldom checked or corrected and her spelling of the words was never re-tested beyond the weekly test. Luckily again, for her, she memorises and retains information like that with little effort. The mere act of looking at the word and reading its definition puts that word at her disposal forever. But she is atypical.

It was because of her memory for spelling that she was being asked to define the words at all. This was an attempt to keep her busy and was not a requirement of most of the other children in her class, who also had a list of unrelated spelling words, but were only vaguely directed to learn them by whatever means they saw fit.

This was a 'good' school, with 'good' teachers, by all accounts. This is vocabulary instruction in this day and age. It's neither vocabulary nor spelling instruction and many children learn next to nothing as a result.

Words studied through their meanings, usage, synonyms, antonyms and etymology are useful. English words heaped together in random lists to be 'learned' solely to pass a spelling test on Friday might as well be in Swahili or Japanese.

Sight word vocabulary (SWV)

Following on from automatic processing, the concept of sight word vocabulary is tricky and can be badly misinterpreted.

The process of placing a word in the SWV differs from the process of retrieving it. There is some overlap, but because a familiar word almost instantly activates the lexical-semantic lexicon, it is easy to overlook the crucial role phonology plays in establishing the word there in the first place.

Linnea Ehri's *orthographic mapping* theory demonstrates clearly what happens when words are processed. Reading is learned efficiently if children have good phonemic awareness and knowledge of the alphabetic code. They are then able to form a 'map' of a word's spelling for easy recall later.

The chapter on teaching vocabulary in the final section of the book addresses this and several other points and has suggestions for further reading and learning on the subject of vocabulary.

References

Beck, I. L., McKeown, M. G., & Kucan, L. (2002). *Bringing Words to Life: Robust Vocabulary Instruction*. New York: GuilfordPress.

Dehaene, S. (2010). *Reading in the Brain: The New Science of How We Read*. New York: Penguin.

Smith, F. (1971). *Understanding Reading: A Psycholinguistic Analysis of Reading and Learning to Read*. New York: Lawrence Erlbaum.

Stanovich, K. E. (1980). Toward an Interactive-Compensatory Model of Individual Differences in the Development of Reading Fluency. *Reading Research Quarterly*, 16(1), 32–71.

Comprehension

From Latin *com* 'with, together' and *prehendere* 'to seize, get hold of'.

Quick quiz:

In a 2014 study of 425,000 first through third graders, decoding, vocabulary and comprehension were all tested (Spencer, Quinn & Wagner 2014). Some children scored low on all three measures. Some scored low on decoding and vocabulary but not comprehension. But there was a percentage of children who scored high on decoding and vocabulary but low on comprehension.

This is the population that some pundits could say are 'barking at print'. In a code-based, systematic scheme of instruction, children are taught to decode *and* comprehend what they read through the process of orthographic mapping. In the psycholinguistic guessing game, so popular in current education, children are taught *not* to decode in case they somehow 'lose meaning'. Can you guess what percentage fell into the band that might need to focus on meaning rather than decoding? 10%? 20%? How many? The answer and discussion are at the end of this chapter.

What is comprehension?

Reading comprehension is a combination of *thought processes*, rather than one teachable skill. It can be assessed by evaluating how well students can recall facts, infer, conclude, predict and find the main idea in increasingly complex texts.

It relies on, and can be impaired by deficits in, the following areas:

- phonological awareness
- word-level reading
- lexical-semantic vocabulary
- syntactical-grammatical knowledge
- working memory
- background knowledge

We have already explored the first three processes. Phonological awareness is essential for rapid, stable learning of the alphabetic code. Effective instruction in this code increases automaticity in word-level reading. Practice and explicit instruction in fluent reading bolsters and adds to the lexical-semantic vocabulary.

Syntactical-grammatical knowledge and working memory will be explored in depth in the next chapter on the underlying processes for reading.

This leaves background knowledge – a key factor in reading comprehension. Unfortunately, it is also a variable that teachers have very little control over in the first few years of schooling.

Children arrive at school with spectacularly varied levels of competence, whether it be due to family circumstances or neurological capability or both. Much debate rages about the correct starting point for literacy teaching in the face of such diversity.

Understandably, many are convinced that comprehension and literary appreciation can and should be taught right from the start, and these people are not wrong. However, the approach that levels the playing field for *all* children is the one that produces the greatest amount of independence in the largest number of children after the second year of teaching.

When I mention independence, I do not simply mean taking a book and reading it to oneself. I mean taking a text and reading it without relying on prediction or pictures. I mean writing about what you experience legibly and with plausible, if not perfect, spelling.

The approach that gives the majority of children this independence is one which systematically emphasises the coded structure of words and the correspondences that the letters on the page have to the sounds of the spoken language.

Quality, high-content, explicit teaching in these years is essential, which is one of the main reasons that low-content, discovery or investigation-based teaching has such a low success rate in raising achievement in schools.

A few things to remember about comprehension

1. Don't confuse the journey with the destination.

    Like word-level automaticity, understanding what you read is the *destination*, not the journey. The journey consists of increasingly strategic use of:
    - oral language
    - phonological awareness
    - phonics
    - fluency
    - vocabulary

2. Guessing is a dead-end street.

   Looking at pictures, predicting words in a story, guessing words, skipping words and trying to use context to get words off the page are actions which do not feature in any of the above keys to reading. They are also poor comprehension strategies which require much more mental effort than simply decoding words and connecting them to oral language.

3. 'Making meaning' is not a thing.

   This phrase is, ironically, meaningless. In linguistics, we talk about semantics and pragmatics. In the science of reading, we talk about decoding and connecting to oral language.

   In the imprecise and evidence-free world of whole language, 'making meaning' is nothing but a catchphrase, and ultimately, an inaccurate approximation of the process of reading comprehension. Inaccurate catchphrases are not good enough if we are to eradicate illiteracy.

4. Decoding is not in direct competition with reading comprehension.

   Decoding leads to and is ultimately inseparable from comprehension. Try reading the word *dog* and resisting its meaning. The concept of dog is immediate and inseparable from the letters <d><o><g>.

   When students lack the skills to decode, clumsily trying to circumvent their deficits by plastering comprehension strategies over the holes is a dreadful thing to do.

Quiz answer

How many children were adequate decoders with adequate vocabularies who scored poorly in tests of reading comprehension?

Fewer than 1% of all children surveyed.

Around one in every hundred children requires explicit comprehension teaching and prompting. So the next time you hear someone using comprehension as a path to word-level reading, ask them if they are dealing with the 1%. If they are not, why are behaving like they are?

Making reading comprehension the primary driver for literacy instruction is considerably less likely to be successful than starting with decoding and/or vocabulary.

Reference

Spencer, M., Quinn, J. M., & Wagner, R. K. (2014), Specific Reading Comprehension Disability: Major Problem, Myth, or Misnomer? *Learning Disabilities Research & Practice*, 29(1), 3–9. doi:10.1111/ldrp.12024

CHAPTER 8

Underlying processes for reading

Up until this point, we have looked at the teachable skills that underlie reading:

- phonological awareness
- phonics
- fluency
- vocabulary

We have also explored some of the related abilities that smooth the process of becoming a reader:

- oral language development
- background knowledge

There are other factors which come into play when learning to read, which, if weak, impair progress. Among these factors are:

- rapid automatized naming (RAN)
- working memory
- processing speed

These three factors are measurable but cannot be directly taught and cannot be significantly improved. This doesn't mean that low scores in any of the above present a hopeless picture. What it does mean, though, is that programs and practitioners that say they can improve RAN, working memory or processing speed in ways that transfer to reading are making claims that are not in any way supported by the current scientific consensus.

In this chapter, we will define and explore examples of low ability in the three processes above and talk about what *can* be done in order to compensate. At this point in time, however, compensation is the only solution known to science.

Rapid automatized naming (RAN)

Imagine that you are on a game show where desirable objects (a toaster, a TV, a giant teddy bear) are shown to you in quick succession on a conveyor belt. Every object you name in a fraction of a second, before it disappears, is yours to keep.

If you win lots of prizes, this basically means you are adept at rapid automatized naming (RAN).

RAN measurement gives important information about how efficiently children are processing the sounds of their language and how well they would respond to small group intervention, should their reading skills be lagging.

A student with phonological deficits and low RAN would progress more slowly and would be a more needful candidate for one-to-one intervention than a student with phonological deficits but average RAN.

Because RAN tests are short, this is an efficient way of predicting reading skill and deciding where and how to place a student in terms of intervention.

As stated before, RAN cannot be directly taught or improved; it is something of a fixed ability. All the coaching in the world will not significantly speed up a person's RAN and any small gains in speed will certainly not transfer to reading.

Working memory

Memory has been a subject of fascination to mankind throughout the ages. There is some agreement among scientists about the different types of memory, roughly divided into short- and long-term categories.

Information that you need to retain, such as your name and where you live, can be said to reside in the long-term memory, whereas remembering to pick up milk on the way home from work only needs to be stored until you pick up the milk, and therefore resides in the short-term memory.

A subcategory of short-term memory is working memory. Once again, you are a participant on a game show, but instead of rapidly naming the toaster, TV, teddy and 22 other items, you have to keep all of them in your mind until the conveyor belt stops moving and the items are out of sight. All items you can name after they're out of sight are yours. How do you think you'd do? How might you do if, while the conveyor belt was moving, a mariachi band was playing in the background and you had to juggle three bananas whilst counting backwards from 1,000? Considerably less well would be the norm.

When reading, working memory gives us the ability to derive meaning from written language. This is where the process of reading becomes so awe-inspiring. To be able to comprehend a text, a person has to do the following things:

- identify the letters rapidly enough to form sequences of sounds in unfamiliar words
- build those sounds into words
- connect those words to oral language
- identify known words rapidly
- access the likely definition of those words based on the context
- accumulate those words to form sentences
- assemble those sentences to form an understanding of the author's intent

The conductor in this orchestra of processes is working memory.

The more distractions there are in the learning environment – like the mariachi band in the game show – the harder it is to learn to read. It is bewildering that primary schools, who bear the greatest responsibility for teaching our children to read, have open-plan classrooms where the noise and movement of other classes can be heard during lessons. Every child with working memory deficits is disadvantaged by this.

Like RAN tests, working memory tests are quick and easy to carry out and give us vital information about helping struggling readers.

There is another important process involved in reading that working memory determines. This is the implicit learning of new words based on context (Kuhn & Stahl 1998).

The Lewis Carroll poem *Jabberwocky* contains words that the author invented, such as *jabberwock*, *galumph*, *brillig* and *snicker-snack*. But they were sufficiently bolstered by words in general usage that most readers know exactly what happened in the poem and, furthermore, can talk to others about the poem using these newly learned words.

We can only be directly taught so many words. In an ideal classroom, teachers have the capacity to teach 300 to 400 words in a school year (Stahl 1991). Yet it is estimated that typically developing children learn up to ten times as many in a year (Graves 1986; White, Graves & Slater 1990). They do this by reading.

However, learning new words this way is much more challenging for children with working memory deficits. They will find the task of holding everything together whilst storing a new word sometimes impossible. The gap between a new word and the information required to understand the meaning of the new word increases this difficulty.

So poor working memory doesn't just slow a reader's pace, it also hinders comprehension and prevents readers from gaining new words for their vocabularies. This in turn loops back to impede fluency and vocabulary. This point is of paramount significance.

Unfortunately, like RAN, an increase in working memory capacity does not transfer directly to an increase in reading skill.

As practitioners, we have to build fixes around working memory. This comes back down to presenting phonetic information systematically and allowing time for practice and overlearning.

This also involves making sure teachers, parents and students themselves know what to expect in terms of pace and the timeframe that it takes to make a proficient reader out of a person whose working memory is low.

Working memory deficits require leaving nothing to chance. Random, embedded phonics is not enough to help children who have low working memory.

The key to proficient reading is ordered, controlled, distraction-free practice, founded on a broad base of letter–sound relationships. This is good for everyone, and especially for those whose working memory is below average.

Processing speed

Some children are naturally fast. They laugh at jokes first, they put their hands up in class first, they finish their work first. These are the fast processors. Rapid naming is beneficial when converting phonological information to semantic information, but processing speed is the ability to *respond* to that information.

There are also those who need a little more time to think things through and get things done. The measure of this ability is called processing speed.

To return to the game show, this time you have to lift items off the conveyor belt and put them into specially designated pigeonholes. Red items go into the blue pigeonhole, blue items go into the green pigeonhole, multicoloured items go into the black pigeonhole and so on. You only get two seconds per item to make your choice. All correctly placed items are yours to take home. In addition to that, if you correctly place an item in under one second, you get an additional cash prize to the value of that item. The entrants who would end up rich and prize-laden would be the fastest processors.

Processing speed is important when learning to read, but low processing speed does not necessarily impair learning to read. It does, however, impair the level of skill a person can attain in reading.

Some children are labelled 'lazy' or 'unmotivated', when, in fact, their processing speed is low.

Working memory can only hold information for brief periods of time, so slow processors will quickly run out of time before the working memory has had a chance to use incoming information properly.

There is no single part of the brain involved with processing speed. Instead, a person's ability to process and respond to information involves a complex network of different brain structures. This is one of the reasons why, once again, like RAN and working memory, processing speed cannot be directly affected in ways that will improve reading.

Some indicators of low processing speed:

- The child seems to repeat parts of a sentence or go back to the beginning of a sentence when speaking.
- The child has difficulty explaining simple concepts.
- The child takes a long time to complete routine tasks.
- The child tends to forget instructions.
- The child becomes overwhelmed by multiple sources of information.
- The child is anxious on the subject of time constraints.

Children with slow processing speed but no deficits in any of the other underlying processes for reading can learn to read in an average timeframe (i.e. in the first three years of schooling). However, reading fluency, once the alphabetic code has been mastered, is heavily impaired by processing speed, which in turn can lead to poor comprehension.

Processing speed can also be affected by anxiety: the more worried a child is, the slower they go, which increases their worry, etc. These children can also become frustrated by and disengaged from schoolwork, especially in a group setting, where they know the answer but can't demonstrate their knowledge quickly enough.

What can be done

If RAN, working memory or processing speed deficits are suspected, a cognitive assessment from an educational psychologist is a crucial starting point. This will provide insight into the areas of difficulty a child has as well as a guide to possible home- and school-based accommodations to help the child reach their potential.

Please beware of any recommendations that include interventions targeting RAN, working memory or processing speed. These are subskills and cannot be increased to a point that directly affects literacy. Explicit teaching and plenty of practice will raise literacy faster, and in most cases, at a much lower cost, than 'brain training' programs aimed at these underlying processes. See the Snake Oil chapter for more on these fraudulent interventions.

References

Graves, M. (1986). Vocabulary Learning and Instruction. *Review of Research in Education*, 13, 49–89.

Kuhn, M. R., & Stahl, S. A. (1998). Teaching Children to Learn Word Meanings from Context: A Synthesis and Some Questions. *Journal of Literacy Research*, 30(1), 119–38. doi:10.1080/10862969809547983

Stahl, S. A. (1991). Beyond the Instrumental Hypothesis: Some Relationships Between Word Meanings and Comprehension. In Schwanenflugel, P. J. (Ed.), *The Psychology of Word Meanings*, pp. 157–85. Hillsdale, NJ: Erlbaum.

White, T. G., Graves, M. F., & Slater, W. H. (1990). Growth of Reading Vocabulary in Diverse Elementary Schools: Decoding and Word Meaning. *Journal of Educational Psychology*, 82(2), 281–90.

CHAPTER 9

The consequences of low literacy

I find housework boring, frustrating, difficult and unpleasant. Therefore, I avoid it. I'm quite happy to live in a messy house. I am fortunate enough to have the wherewithal to pay someone else to do the necessary tasks to ensure it is at least clean. I don't worry about losing out on vital housework practice; more housework does not improve my ability to do housework. I have no shame in admitting I avoid housework.

Avoiding what you don't like is a natural human act. But imagine not liking reading. It's hard to live in a complex society without being able to and very few can pay others to do their reading for them. Reading avoidance leads to low progress in reading and, in turn, in other academic subjects. Along with the social and economic disadvantages of low literacy, there is also the shame. Not liking reading is very different from not liking housework.

The school-to-prison pipeline

I remember once being staggered by a simple correlation, presented by Professor Kerry Hempenstall, in a lecture about dyslexia. He said that several states in the US based their prison projections on primary school reading scores.

Newspaper reports have told of prison contractors in California and Arizona, to name but two, predicting the number of prison beds needed up to ten years ahead by looking at the number of children who couldn't read by the fourth year of school (Schmoker 1999; Block & Weisz 2004).

The term *school-to-prison pipeline* was coined by social justice commentators in the US to explain the link between exclusion of students of colour from school and their eventual involvement with the criminal justice system. It has since been adopted elsewhere to describe other links between poor educational practice and crime.

Like any social phenomenon, factors leading to criminal activity are many and complex, but low literacy can be, as many in the field have pointed out, 'the first link in a causal chain' towards negative life circumstances, including crime and incarceration (Morgan, Farkas & Wu 2012).

Shame fatigue

Prison statistics the world over show that the majority of inmates have no or low ability to read. Turning to crime is an understandable result of not being employable, as is 'shame fatigue', the term coined by psychologist and leading light in the field of reading research, Steven Dykstra. Here he describes the experience of many of the thousands of struggling readers he has seen over his career:

> A kid, a teenager who started out as an unrecognized, untreated victim of dyslexia and probably some other learning issues, eventually graduated up to truancy, drugs, and a bunch of other stuff. When we talked about it, this child helped me see the pathway that leads to that decline, and it centers on shame.
>
> Shame is supposed to keep us from doing certain things. We may have the impulse or the opportunity, but shame stops us. But if you're a dyslexic kid, getting no help, working hard every day to keep your dyslexia hidden and unnoticed, terrified you're just stupid and everyone is going to figure it out at any moment, you have been drenched in shame your whole life. Shame has become so familiar to you that when you get older and the opportunities are there to do things you shouldn't, shame doesn't really have much effect anymore. Shame is no big deal, it's a constant, just part of your life.
>
> I think that is the vector by which a lot of our kids take a header later in their school years, when they have shame fatigue and it just doesn't matter anymore.
>
> (Personal communication)

So much shame and poor behaviour could be avoided through high quality early reading instruction, early identification of language impairment and effective intervention.

This is not to say that poor behaviour should be tolerated. Far from it. Schools that develop a strong culture of high expectations of proper conduct and which consistently reinforce consequences for misconduct are bound to do better than schools which allow or make excuses for bad behaviour.

Mental health and literacy

There are many children who have enough financial and family support to avoid crime, but whose struggles with reading still come at a great cost.

In the paper *Do Poor Readers Feel Angry, Sad, and Unpopular?*, researchers Morgan, Farkas and Wu concluded that the evidence is strongly supportive of the hypothesis in the title.

Many studies have shown that traits such as

- frustration,
- distractibility,
- social isolation,
- agitation,
- withdrawal, and
- aggression

are common among struggling readers. Though it is almost impossible to establish causal links between the two, illiteracy and social maladjustment are unmistakably inter-related.

Teenage pregnancy is prevalent among illiterate girls. Drug abuse and suicide are also overly represented by people who can't read.

All of this is understandable. If you can't read, your life choices are very different from those of literate people. It is hard to fit into or contribute to society. Illiteracy is *everybody's* problem. The costs of crime, poor mental health, unwanted children and drug abuse affect everyone.

There is much talk in education about '21st century skills' and 'preparing for jobs that haven't been invented yet', but we need to get the basics of literacy and numeracy right before flying off into a futuristic fantasy world. Professor Pamela Snow has spent much of her career examining the links between literacy and social justice. She summarises this situation well:

> *This shift in workforce composition and opportunities for engagement in the economic mainstream stands to disadvantage students who exit school with poorly developed oral language and literacy skills. It also reinforces the importance of maximising the quality of the early instructional environment so that all, not just most children, successfully make the transition to literacy and can fully access opportunities for further educational advancement.*

(29)

References

Block, A., & Weisz, V. (2004). Choosing Prisoners Over Pupils. *The Washington Post*, 6 July. http://www.washingtonpost.com/wp-dyn/articles/A29806-2004Jul5.html?noredirect=on

Morgan, P. L., Farkas, G., & Wu, Q. (2012). Do Poor Readers Feel Angry, Sad, and Unpopular? *Scientific Studies of Reading: The Official Journal of the Society for the Scientific Study of Reading*, 16(4), 360–81. http://doi.org/10.1080/10888438.2011.570397

Schmoker, M. (1999). The Quiet Revolution in Achievement. *Education Week*, 3 November. https://www.edweek.org/ew/articles/1999/11/03/10schmoker.h19.html

Snow, P. C. (2016). Elizabeth Usher Memorial Lecture: Language is Literacy is Language: Positioning Speech-Language Pathology in Education Policy, Practice, Paradigms and Polemics. *International Journal of Speech-Language Pathology*, 18(3), 216–28. doi:10.3109/17549507.2015.1112837

CHAPTER 10

The major players

In early times, reading was mostly taught through different variations of phonics. However, disagreement about the process of reading and the method of teaching it existed among scholars as far back as the 18th century. One of the strongest theories competing against phonics was the whole word approach.

Advocates of this method argued that since people spoke in whole words, they should also learn to read in whole words, and not in a 'parts-to-whole' manner. Despite the success of phonics, whole word crept into schools and phonics began losing ground.

Whole word methods had attracted firm and powerful adherents who helped flood the market with supporting resources.

Illiteracy soared wherever whole word methods took hold, and even though researchers proved phonics to be superior to whole word, it wasn't until Rudolf Flesch's groundbreaking 1955 book *Why Johnny Can't Read* was released, that the pendulum began to swing back in favour of phonics.

Pendulum swings were all very well, but as the 20th century marched on, the importance of phonics as a foundation of literacy acquisition became undeniable through the research of scholars in psychology, linguistics and education. This did not deter certain theorists from coming up with a third theory and starting an educational revolution that we are still reeling from.

The theory was, of course, whole language.

Whole language is based upon an attractive, but demonstrably false assumption:

> *Children learn to speak naturally by simple immersion in language, therefore, children learn to read by the same process.*

A theory like that in a post-1960s world, where personal freedom, individuality and breaking away from structure, discipline and authority were the norm, inevitably resulted in those ideas being taken up by society quickly and readily.

'Let the children play!' was suddenly the coolest thing to say in education. The battle still rages on between those known as traditional and progressive educationalists.

Each major branch of reading theory – whole word, whole language and phonics – had its adherents setting out to prove their views correct.

Two significant things happened which brought us to where we are today:

1. Researchers in the fields of linguistics, psychology, neurology, speech pathology and education began testing the various theories and communicating their findings.
2. Business people began developing products and programs to sell to schools.

And like two paths in a wood, science and business diverged.

Who's who of reading

This Reading Wars story is long, complicated and continuing. There is much further reading that can be done to help understand its intricacies. Rather than re-hash the entire thing, I have provided a table to help readers see at a glance who is who. The table contains some biographical details and key ideas/publications by the major players in the story.

Throughout my career, the same names have appeared over and over again, and I've often wondered who these people are. They are listed here in alphabetical order in Table 10.1.

Thousands of research documents on reading are written every year in dozens of languages. This chart is by no means an exhaustive list of every single contributor to the field. It has been checked by various highly knowledgeable editors for glaring omissions, but omissions are inevitable. Appeals for inclusion of anyone I've missed in subsequent editions would be welcomed.

The people on this list have had long and distinguished careers that defy limitation to one or two paragraphs, but nonetheless, I have tried to pinpoint the concepts that they are best known for coining and/or developing.

Similarly, I have had to limit their major publications to one or two. Some have authored and co-authored dozens of books and papers.

Table 10.1 The major players in reading instruction

Name	Born	Field	Big Idea (s)	Notable publications
Richard Allington	1947	Education research	Special education creates illiterate people. 'Balanced literacy' is the perfect antidote to the 'one-size-fits-all' approach of systematic, direct instruction.	*Reading Instruction that Works: The Case for Balanced Teaching (2014)*
Richard C. Anderson	1934	Educational Psychology	Influential researcher on the link between children's reading and their vocabulary growth	• *(Chair) Becoming a Nation of Readers: The Report of the Commission on Reading (1985)*
Elsa Auerbach	c. 1946	Applied linguistics	Education and social justice are inextricably linked.	• *Making Meaning, Making Change (1992)*
Isabel Beck	c. 1932	Education research	Vocabulary instruction can be guided by categorizing words into three tiers (see Vocabulary chapter for more information).	• *Bringing Words to Life: Robust Vocabulary Instruction (2013)*
Dorothy Bishop	1952	Psychology and developmental language impairment	Language impairment has a strong genetic component.	• *Language development in exceptional circumstances (1988)* • *Handedness and developmental disorders (1990)* • *Uncommon understanding (1997)*
Benjamin Bloom	1913	Psychology	Bloom's Taxonomy: a hierarchy of educational goals	• *Taxonomy of Educational Objectives (1956)* • *All Our Children Learning (1980)*
Caroline Bowen	1944	Speech–Language Pathology	One of the more eminent contributors to the field in the subject of evidence-based practice vs. pseudoscience	• *Children's Speech Sound Disorders (2015)* • *Making Sense of Interventions for Children with Developmental Disorders (2017)*

(continued)

Table 10.1 Continued

Name	Born	Field	Big Idea (s)	Notable publications
Brian Cambourne	c. 1935	Education	Author of the 'Conditions of Learning' model which is based on a constructivist theory of education. It has often been erroneously applied to the teaching of reading. This model does not include essential elements of evidence-based instruction and adheres to the discredited notion that all children will learn to read if immersed in a text-rich environment. Cambourne famously described explicit instruction as 'readicide'.	• *(& Kiggins, J.) Reforming how we prepare teachers to teach literacy: Why? What? How? (2013)*
Anne Castles	1964	Cognitive science	The diverse nature of developmental dyslexia and causes and treatment of different types of dyslexia	• *(& Coltheart) Varieties of developmental dyslexia (1993)* • *Orthographic Processes in Reading (2008)*
Jeanne Chall	1921	Psychology & literacy research	Direct, explicit, systematic phonics Readability calculations Beginning reading is different from expert reading	• *Learning to Read the Great Debate (1967)* • *Stages of Reading Development (1983)* • *The Academic Challenge: What Really Works in the Classroom (2000)*
James Chapman	1948	Psychology	Reading Recovery has not served its native country, New Zealand well.	• *(& William Tunmer) Excellence and equity in literacy education: the case of New Zealand (2015)*
Carol Chomsky	1930	Linguistics	'Repeated Reading', where a child silently reads a passage accompanied by a recording of the passage being read. This was said to enhance reading fluency.	*The Acquisition of Syntax in Children From 5 to 10 (1969)*

(continued)

Table 10.1 Continued

Name	Born	Field	Big Idea (s)	Notable publications
Marie Clay	1926	Psychology	Reading Recovery remedial literacy program, which became widely used in English-speaking countries and has been heavily (and largely detrimentally) influential on reading theory and teaching practice. In the past two decades, Reading Recovery has been shown to be ineffective for many children, which many researchers attribute to its lack of a systematic synthetic phonics component.	• *Reading Recovery: A guidebook for teachers in training* (1993)
Max Coltheart	1939	Cognitive sicence	The 'Dual Route' theory of reading (sounding out + word recognition from memory) The two-factor theory of delusional belief	• *(& Rastle, K., Perry, C., Langdon, R., & Ziegler, J.). DRC: A Dual Route Cascaded model of visual word recognition and reading aloud. (2001)*
Andrew Davis		Philosophy of Education	A vocal opponent of phonics (though he says he is not) and is often quoted in arguments for whole language.	• *To read or not to read: Decoding synthetic phonics (2013)*
Ron Davis	1942	Business	One of the most well known proponents of a non evidence-based approach to developmental disorders of reading. It is called the Davis Method.	• *The Gift of Dyslexia (1994)*
Stanislas Dehaene	1965	Cognitive neuroscience	That reading relies on activation of the 'visual word form' area of the brain, which is in turn built by exposure to individual letters and their sounds (i.e. not whole words and certainly not contextual clues).	• *Reading in the Brain (2009)*

(continued)

Table 10.1 Continued

Name	Born	Field	Big Idea (s)	Notable publications
			"Neuronal recycling": how the brain's circuitry borrows from areas normally associated with object recognition and begins to recognize letters and larger linguistic units. This disproves the theory that children are pre-wired to acquire literacy in the same way that they are pre-wired to acquire oral language.	
John Dewey	1859	Psychology	One of the first major proponents of progressive education. His view of "experiential learning" produced fertile ground for whole language and progressive education.	• *My Pedagogic Creed (1897)* • *Experience and Education (1937)*
Katherine Dougherty Stahl	1954	Education	Translating research into practice; early comprehension and assessment	• *(& McKenna, M.C.) Assessment for Reading Instruction (2015)* • *Developing Reading Comprehension: Effective Instruction for All Students in K-2 (2015)*
Linnea Ehri	1941	Educational psychology	Beginning readers form connections between the spellings of individual words and their pronunciations.	• *Research on Learning to Read and Spell: A Personal-Historical Perspective (1997)*

(continued)

Table 10.1 Continued

Name	Born	Field	Big Idea (s)	Notable publications
Siegfried Engelmann	1931	Philosophy and education research	Direct Instruction: explicit, systematic scripted teaching of a particular set of principles Zig was the major architect of Project Follow Through, the largest experiment in education ever conducted. Its findings clearly indicated Direct Instruction as superior to all other methods. Zig is also the co-founder of the National Institute for Direct Instruction (NIFDI)	• *Project Follow Through (1968)* • *Teach your Child to Read in 100 Easy Lessons (1999)*
Rudolph Flesch	1911	Author	That the 'look-say' method of learning to read is inferior to phonics.	• *Why Johnny Can't Read (1955)* • *Why Johnny Still Can't Read: a new look at the scandal of our schools (1981)*
Barbara Foorman	c. 1949	Education research	Professor Foorman is one of those researchers whose work has covered a vast array of reading theory and which has driven the great engine of progress in understanding literacy acquisition. To reduce her to one or two big ideas would be a disservice.	• *Preventing and Remediating Reading Difficulties: Bringing Science to Scale (2003)*
Uta Frith	1941	Cognitive science	The four stages of acquisition of written language	• *The Learning Brain. Lessons for Education (2005)*
Susan Gathercole	1958	Cognitive and behavioural neuroscience	How working memory deficits affect literacy acquisition and what can realistically be done about it	• (& Alloway, T.P.) *Working Memory and Learning: A practical guide for teachers (2008)*
Anna Gillingham	1878	Educational psychology	Sequential, systematic, multi-sensory phonics Syllable types	• *Remedial Training for Children with Specific Disability in Reading, Spelling and Penmanship (1935)*

(continued)

Table 10.1 Continued

Name	Born	Field	Big Idea (s)	Notable publications
Ken Goodman	1921	Education	Reading is a 'psycholinguistic guessing game'.	• What's Whole in Whole Language (1986)
Usha Goswami	1960	Cognitive developmental neuroscience	The neural basis for developmental disorders of literacy and language	• The Wiley-Blackwell Handbook of Childhood Cognitive Development (2010)
Philip Gough	1934	Cognitive science	The Simple View of Reading	• Acquisition of literacy: a longitudinal study of children in first and second grade (1986) • Decoding, reading, and reading disability (1986) • Some observations on a simple view of reading (1996)
William S. Gray	1885	Education	One of the key proponents of the whole word and silent reading methods of literacy instruction.	• On Their Own on Reading (1948)
Peg Griffin	unknown	Applied linguistics	A contributor to the research on reading acquisition since the seventies	• (Editor) Knowledge to Support the Teaching of Reading: Preparing Teachers for a Changing World (2005)
Priscilla Griffith	c. 1947	Education research	Researcher, writer and lecturer with a particular focus on teacher education	• (& Beach, S. A., Ruan, J., & Dunn, L.) Literacy for Young Children: A Guide for Early Childhood Educators (2008)
Patrick Groff	1924	Education	A whole language teacher trainer, until conferring with Jeanne Chall in 1968 and understanding the critical importance of explicit instruction in the alphabetic code. Groff wrote several books and hundreds of papers on the subject of direct instruction.	• Preventing Reading Failure : An Examination of the Myths of Reading Instruction (1987)

(continued)

Table 10.1 Continued

Name	Born	Field	Big Idea (s)	Notable publications
Diana Hanbury-King	1927	Education	Founder of the Academy of Orton-Gillingham Practitioners and Educators	• *A Guide to Helping Your Child at Home: Developing Foundational Skills in Reading and Writing* (2015)
Kerry Hempenstall	1946	Educational Psychology	One of the keepers of all the details relating to the great debate. If contacted and asked for a reference on a particular subject, Professor Hempenstall can almost instantly provide lists of material from his archives that make Google look like amateurs.	• *The three-cueing system in reading: Will it ever go away?* (blog post 2013)
E.D. Hirsch	1928	Education reform	Romantic, anti-intellectual theories of child education, favouring progressive models, are the major cause of academic decline and social inequality. Core knowledge can and should be taught systematically and sequentially rather than 'discovered' through play etc.	• *The Schools We Need and Why We Don't Have Them* (1996) • *The Knowledge Deficit: Closing the Shocking Education Gap for American Children* (2006)
Don Holdaway	1930	Psychology	Founder of the 'big book' and 'shared reading' ideas prevalent in whole language classrooms His disproven theory, that children learn to read by repeatedly experiencing the same text, is called the 'Natural Learning Model'.	• *The Foundations of Literacy* (1984)
Charles Hume	1953	Psychology	Working alongside his wife, another giant in the field, Maggie Snowling, Snowling and Hulme produced a great many books and papers on the subject of literacy, learning and dyslexia.	• *Phonological Abilities Test* (1997) • *The Science of Reading: A Handbook* (2005) • *Developmental Disorders of Language Learning and Cognition* (2009)

(continued)

Table 10.1 Continued

Name	Born	Field	Big Idea (s)	Notable publications
Marilyn Jager Adams	1948	Psychology	Most American children cannot name or write all of the letters of the alphabet by the time they enter second grade. Changing this will raise literacy standards.	• *Beginning to Read: Thinking and Learning About Print (2013)* • *ABC Foundations For Young Children (2013)*
Connie Juel	unknown	Educational psychology	Urged caution when teaching early decoding skills to make sure that oral language and vocabulary development were also a focus.	• *(co-authorship with M. Graves, b. Dewitz) Teaching Reading in the 21st Century (2011)*
David Kilpatrick	c. 1964	Psychology	Kilpatrick has brought the relatively new concept of 'orthographic mapping' to light.	• *Essentials of Assessing, Preventing and Overcoming Reading Difficulties (2015)*
Stephen Krashen	1941	Linguistics	Reading books, not 'heavy' phonics teaches children to read. Krashen attempted to apply his knowledge of second language acquisition to learning to read, but the mismatch has led to an anti systematic synthetic phonics stance.	• *Does Phonics Deserve the Credit for Improvement in PIRLS? (2017)*
Isabelle Liberman	1918	Psychology	The *alphabetic principle* and how this relates to phonological awareness in reading	• *Segmentation of the Spoken Word and Reading Acquisition (1973)*
Patricia Lindamood	1923	Speech and language pathology	One of the first people in the field to build assessment and intervention around phonemic awareness (which she called auditory discrimination)	• *The Lindamood Phoneme Sequencing Program (1998)*

(continued)

Table 10.1 Continued

Name	Born	Field	Big Idea (s)	Notable publications
Maureen Lovett	unknown	Developmental and educational psychology	Leading research in "treatment-resisters", i.e. those who struggle to read despite high quality intervention	• (&Lacerenza, L., Borden, S. L., Frijters, J.C., Steinbach, K.A., & De Palma, M.) *Components of effective remediation for developmental reading disability: Combining phonological and strategy-based instruction to improve outcomes* (2000) • (& Frijters, J.C., Steinbach, K.A., Wolf, M., Sevcik, R.A., & Morris, R.D.) *Early intervention for children at risk for reading disability: The impact of grade at intervention and individual differences on intervention outcomes* (2017)
G. Reid Lyon	1952	Neuroscience	Dr Lyon's research has succeeded in translating scientific findings into real action at the policy-making level. He has been the effective bridge between research and practice in the modern era.	• (& Riccards. P., Blaunstein, P) *Why kids can't read: Challenging the status quo in education.* 2015)
Bruce McCandliss	c. 1968	Neuroscience	Experiments showing that beginning readers who focus on letter-sound relationships, or phonics, increase activity in the area of their brains best wired for reading.	• (& Yoncheva, Y. & Wise, J.) *Hemispheric specialization for visual words is shaped by attention to sublexical units during initial learning* (2015)
Diane McGuinness	1933	Cognitive psychology	Not all phonics is created equal: synthetic phonics is superior. 'Code overlap': symbols can stand for more than one sound. Dyslexia results from a complex code, poorly taught.	• *Why Our Children Can't Read, and What We Can Do about It* (1997) • *Early Reading Instruction: What Science Really Tells Us about How to Teach Reading* (2004)

(continued)

Table 10.1 Continued

Name	Born	Field	Big Idea (s)	Notable publications
Louisa Moats	1944	Psychology	How spelling supports reading How popular, but pseudoscientific ideas in teaching reading can be avoided	• *Speech to Print; Straight Talk About Reading (2000)* • *Basic Facts About Dyslexia (2008)* • *LETRS (Language Essentials for Teachers of Reading and Spelling) professional development program for teachers*
William Nagy	c. 1949	Linguistics	Helped develop the idea that teaching vocabulary improves comprehension.	• *Teaching Vocabulary to Improve Reading Comprehension (1989)* • *(& Steven A. Stahl) Teaching Word Meanings (2006)*
Samuel Orton	1879	Medicine	One of the first individuals to identify and classify what is known as dyslexia Proponent of multisensory structured literacy lessons	• *Reading, Writing and Speech Problems in Children: A presentation of certain types of disorders in the development of the language faculty (1931)*
David Pearson	c. 1942	Education	Reading comprehension involves interaction between the reader, the text and the context. Therefore too much (whatever that means, as Pearson has consistently failed to quantify it) attention to the text and not the 'meaning-making' qualities of the reader, result in poor reading scores.	• *Comprehension Going Forward and What Every Teacher Should Need Know About Reading Comprehension Instruction (2011)*
Charles Perfetti	c. 1937	Psychology	The Lexical Quality Hypothesis: That comprehension skill relies on word-reading skill, not the other way round	• *(& Verhoeven, L.) Learning to read across languages and writing systems (2017)*

(continued)

Table 10.1 Continued

Name	Born	Field	Big Idea (s)	Notable publications
Jean Piaget	1896	Psychology	Children learn through physical interaction with their world (hence constructivism)	• *Science of education and the psychology of the child (1970)*
Sir Jim Rose	1939	Education	Independent reviewer for the UK government. Promotes systematic synthetic phonics.	• *Independent Review of the Teaching of Early Reading. a.k.a. The Rose Report (2006)*
Mark Seidenberg	1953	Psycholinguistics	One of the modern researchers helping to refine our understanding of the nature of skilled reading, reading acquisition and impairments to reading	• *Reading at the Speed of Sight (2016)*
Timothy Shanahan	1951	Reading research	Learning to read and learning to write is a connected process and not something to be taught in isolation.	• *(& Lonigan, C.J.) Early Childhood Literacy: The National Early Literacy Panel and Beyond (2013)*
Donald Shankweiler	c. 1930	Psychology/cognitive science	Researcher investigating the neural basis for developmental problems of speech and reading	• *Reading and phonological processing (2012)*
Sally Shaywitz	c. 1943	Paediatric medicine	Co-founder of the Yale Center for Dyslexia and Creativity, Dr Shaywitz has led the field in refinement of research pertaining to dyslexia for many decades.	• *Overcoming Dyslexia (2003)*
Linda Siegel	1942	Psychology	Another example of a research powerhouse, responsible for hundreds of journal articles further refining the process of reading and reading impairment	• *Not Stupid, Not Lazy: Understanding Dyslexia and Other Learning Disabilities (2016)*
Frank Smith	1928	Psycholinguistics	Founder of the modern whole language approach to reading instruction	• *Understanding Reading: A Psycholinguistic Analysis of Reading and Learning to Read (2004)*

(continued)

Table 10.1 Continued

Name	Born	Field	Big Idea (s)	Notable publications
Catherine Snow	1945	Psychology/ applied linguistics	The way in which social factors contribute to literacy	• *(& Burns, C. & Griffin, P.) Preventing Reading Difficulties in Young Children (1998)* • *Preparing Our Teachers: Opportunities for Better Reading Instruction (2002)*
Pamela Snow	1960	Psychology/speech pathology	The impact that oral language and literacy have on juvenile mental health and social justice	• *(& Bowen, C.) Making Sense of Interventions for Children's Developmental Disorders: A Guide for Parents and Professionals (2017)*
Margaret Snowling	1955	Psychology	Has written and researched extensively on the subject of literacy, learning and especially dyslexia. She and her husband, Charles Hulme, have co-authored many well-known publications on these subjects.	• *Dyslexia, Speech and Language (2006)*
Romalda Spalding	1899	Education	Student of Samuel Orton. Wrote a phonics-based, total language arts program based on how children learn to read and write.	• *The Writing Road to Reading 6th Edition (1957)*
Keith Stanovich	1950	Applied psychology and human development	The Matthew Effect in education 'Dysrationalia': the presence of irrational thinking and action despite adequate intelligence	• *Progress in Understanding Reading: Scientific Foundations and New Frontiers (2000)*

(continued)

Table 10.1 Continued

Name	Born	Field	Big Idea (s)	Notable publications
Robert Sweet	1937	Education policy	U.S. government advisor responsible for writing research proven application of reading science into U.S. law Founder of the National Right to Read Foundation Founding member of the International Foundation for Effective Reading Instruction (IFERI)	• *(& Lyon, G.R.) Reading First (2002)*
Joseph Torgesen	1943	Developmental Psychology	Another research powerhouse whose work spans many and varied subjects, but chief contributor to notions of characteristics of effective instruction for children with reading disabilities.	• *Co-author of the Comprehensive test of Phonological Processes (CTOPP 2013)* • *Test of Word Reading Efficiency (TOWRE 2012)*
Rebecca Treiman	1954	Child developmental psychology	Research on writing systems and how they are learned and used	• *How Children Learn to Write Words (2014)*
William Tunmer		Educational psychology	Powerhouse researcher on early literacy development, literacy learning difficulties, and reading intervention	• *(& Chapman, J.) Excellence and equity in literacy education: the case of New Zealand (2015)*
Frank Vellutino	c. 1935	Psychology	Assessment and explanation of core deficits in perception that lead to delayed literacy acquisition	• *Dyslexia Theory and Research (1981)*
Richard Venezky	1938	Education research	Groundbreaking researcher in the field of literacy and learning whose work with computers helped to provide a strong theoretical basis for the argument that English spelling is predictable and regular and has spelling to sound patterns that help in learning to read.	• *The American Way of Spelling: The structure and origins of American English Orthography (1999)*

(continued)

Table 10.1 Continued

Name	Born	Field	Big Idea (s)	Notable publications
Lev Vygotsky	1896	Psychology	Coined the 'zone of proximal development' theory and was a major influence in the 'learning through play' movement still popular in schools (though his works may have been distorted and misinterpreted to fit progressive education views).	• *Play and its role in the Mental development of the Child (1933)*
Kevin Wheldall	1949	Educational Psychology/ Special Education	Writer and researcher of scientific evidence-based reading interventions for young struggling readers and older low-progress readers (and latterly beginning readers) Founder of Making Up Lost Time in Literacy (MultiLit)	• *(& Beaman, R.) An evaluation of MultiLit (2000)* • *Effective instruction for socially disadvantaged low-progress readers: The Schoolwise program (2008)*
Daniel Willingham	1961	Psychology	Debunking the 'Learning Styles' myth The importance of knowledge in driving reading comprehension	• *Why Don't Students Like School (2009)*
Maryanne Wolf	1947	Cognitive neuroscience	Research into the role that rapid automatized naming (RAN) plays in literacy acquisition	• *Proust and the Squid: The Story and Science of the Reading Brain (2007)*

CHAPTER 11

Children left behind

I have concluded that the federal government here in the US is not the place for significant reform.

Robert Sweet

Promising to raise standards in education is a common political platform. This is one of the main reasons why there have been several major inquiries into the teaching of reading worldwide in the last two decades.

An inquiry consists of submissions and hearings taken from experts and stakeholders in the field. Information is gathered, analysed, collated and a report and recommendations are composed.

An inquiry is convened so that policy makers can understand as deeply and as rapidly as possible, the situation at hand, what can be done to improve it, and the best methods of bringing about that improvement.

Quick quiz:

What percentage of the three major inquiries in the US, the UK and Australia since 1998 do you think recommended *not* teaching the alphabetic code early, systematically and explicitly?

What percentage concluded that whole language or whole word approaches would be most effective in raising literacy?

Zero.

This and the next two chapters will detail those inquiries and seek to answer the question: *If we know so much about teaching reading, why do so many leave school illiterate?*

[handwritten: Because this info doesn't get to teachers in the trenches.]

The Snow Report (Preventing Reading Difficulties in Young Children)

In 1998, as a reaction to static reading scores across the US, the National Academy of Sciences, a non-profit society of distinguished scholars, commissioned one of the best-known documents in the field. This became known as *The Snow Report.* Its full title was *Preventing Reading Difficulties in Young Children.*

The report was written by Catherine Snow, Susan Burns and Peg Griffin (see Table 10.1) and was a clearly written literature review.

In summary, the report identified:

- '... the conditions under which reading is most likely to develop easily' and provided
- 'recommendations for practice as well as recommendations for further research.'

Its ten sections were listed as follows:

1. Introduction (detailing the process of literature review and expert panel hearings)
2. The process of learning to read
3. Who has reading difficulties
4. Predictors of success and failure in reading
5. Preventing reading difficulties before kindergarten
6. Instructional strategies for kindergarten and the primary grades
7. Organisational strategies for kindergarten and the primary grades
8. Helping children with reading difficulties in grades 1–3
9. The agents of change
10. Recommendations for practice and research

The authors' focus was prevention. They listened to presentations from a diverse range of researchers and practitioners in the field. They gathered as many strands of the professional literature as they could in order to present an unbiased, factual account of how best to teach reading. Their conclusion was that the alphabetic code had to be taught from the first year of school and children needed regular, systematic practice to gain mastery in phonics, vocabulary, fluency and comprehension. Who would have thought it?

Representatives of whole language and whole word approaches were also listened to and their theories were held up to scrutiny. The authors concluded:

'Although context and pictures can be used as a tool to monitor word recognition, children should not be taught to use them to substitute for information provided by the letters in the word.'

The National Reading Panel

In 1962 the US government established the National Institute for Child Health and Human Development (NIHCD) as a part of the National Institutes of Health (NIH). Its purpose was to 'investigate human development throughout the entire life process'.

The Child Development and Behavior Branch, headed by eminent psychologist Dr Reid Lyon, oversaw funding for 'research and research training relevant to the psychological, neurobiological, language, behavioral, and educational development and health of children' at many major universities in the US.

In 1997, Dr Lyon was asked by the US Congress to oversee a national panel to look into what was known about reading and to formulate a report that:

- '... should present the panel's conclusions',
- 'an indication of the readiness for application in the classroom of the results of this research, and, if appropriate',
- 'a strategy for rapidly disseminating this information to facilitate effective reading instruction in the schools.'
- 'If found warranted, the panel should also recommend a plan for additional research regarding early reading development and instruction.'

The panel was named the National Reading Panel (NRP). The Snow Report was used as a foundational document, but added to that were regional public hearings and the establishment of six subgroups. These were:

1. Alphabetics
2. Comprehension
3. Fluency
4. Methodology
5. Teacher Education
6. Technology/Next Steps

Once again, the findings of the panel concerning normal reading development, reading disabilities and developmental disorders of language converged on the importance of early alphabetic code instruction. At no time did looking at pictures, memorising whole words or using contextual guessing enter the recommendations (see National Reading Panel 2000).

The Reading Excellence Act

The NIHCD research had a major influence on government policy and received bi-partisan support. Bill Clinton's 1998 Reading Excellence Act was influenced by this (see Civic Impulse 2018). Its goal it was to ensure that 'all children read well and independently by the end of third grade'.

The act also made clear that many children with reading difficulties could catch up without specialist tutoring if early screening and improved teacher quality were made a priority – early echoes of the Response to Intervention (RTI) model, more about which will follow.

States all over America began developing proposals in order to receive grants. The act stated:

> 'Mastering the skills of phonemic awareness, systematic phonics, and reading comprehension are essential if students are to become fluent readers.'

The ensuing *Report of the National Reading Panel* was distributed to every elementary school in the US by 2002.

The No Child Left Behind bill

After Clinton came Bush, and though the political party changed, the political will to raise literacy standards in the US remained the same. Reid Lyon, Robert Sweet and their colleagues continued to provide high quality research and advice, resulting in the No Child Left Behind (NCLB) bill. This became law in 2002.

The *Reading First* and *Early Reading First* sections of the NCLB provided funding for and training in the five keys components of reading instruction.

Lyon and Sweet defined the term *scientifically based reading research* as quantitative research, and that definition became part of US education law.

The law also focused on holding schools accountable for student outcomes. It was an excellent, if ambitious, plan.

The story is best told in the words of Robert Sweet, who generously gave an interview for this book:

> 'I think this is likely the largest and most comprehensive campaign for improving reading instruction in the history of the US.
>
> 'However, the result was marginalised because the United States Department of Education did not follow through with the intent of the Reading First legislation, and did not hold states accountable for changing the way reading was being taught in the local schools.
>
> 'As is often the case, the power of money superseded the desire to really help improve reading instruction. The Reading First law was dependent on states and local communities wanting to change the paradigm of how

reading was taught. That did not occur in many instances. However, in states where it did work, thousands of teachers were presented with the findings of reading science.

'It is difficult to maintain momentum on changing deeply held beliefs. The whole word juggernaut that had been underway for more than a half century since the days of John Dewey was not easily deterred. In 2005, the US Office for Management and Budget noted that "Reading First" was one of three recently approved laws that was making a "measurable" difference in student achievement in reading. For a variety of political reasons, NCLB was not reauthorised and thus went the way of so many other national initiatives of merit.

'Was it worth the effort? I would say it was, as the reverberations continue to resonate with many because the job remains undone.

'Now we are nearly two decades away from this initiative, the test scores remain abysmally bad, especially for our minority students. 84% of African Americans students still graduate from high school unable to read proficiently, and the situation is the same for Hispanic students. More than 60% of all US students still cannot read proficiently. A tragedy for them for sure, and that is why we all continue to try and think through ways to address this issue as best we can.'

The National Right to Read Foundation

Robert Sweet co-founded and became the president of the National Right to Read Foundation (NRRF) in 1993 and remains there to this day. This non-profit organisation has one mission:

'Returning scientifically validated classroom instruction in reading to America's public school classrooms.'

And by *scientifically validated instruction* they mean:

'... systematic, direct instruction in phonemic awareness, phonics, vocabulary development, fluency and comprehension ...'.

Interestingly, there are few other non-profit foundations in the US dedicated to putting guessing, looking at pictures, inferring from context or learning lists of whole words into America's public school classrooms. The drivers behind the existing unproven and non-scientific ideas and practices are big publishing companies, big unions and even bigger profits.

Robert Sweet, Reid Lyon and the countless other campaigners for reading reform in the US continue to unite, advance and support the efforts of reading researchers and professionals the world over.

But even with their academic prowess and political connections, they will be unable to make significant changes for the better without a groundswell of public demand. As a solution to this problem, Robert became a founding member of the *International Foundation for Effective Reading Instruction* (IFERI) and the *Coalition for Reading Excellence* in the US.

References

Civic Impulse. (2018). H.R. 2614 — 105th Congress: Reading Excellence Act. https://www.govtrack.us/congress/bills/105/hr2614

National Reading Panel. (2000). *Teaching Children to Read: An Evidence-Based Assessment of the Scientific Literature on Reading and Its Implications for Reading Instruction—Reports of the Subgroups*. Washington, DC: Author.

National Research Council. (1998). *Preventing Reading Difficulties in Young Children*. Washington, DC: The National Academies Press. https://doi.org/10.17226/6023

CHAPTER 12

Rose to the occasion

The British story is fairly complicated, in that sometimes laws regarding education include England only and other times they are enacted nationally to encompass Scotland, Wales and Northern Ireland as well.

Literacy levels in all four nations vary, with England at the top and Wales at the bottom. Much activism is afoot in Scotland under the guidance of Anne Glennie, who in 2017 lodged a parliamentary petition to:

> ... urge the Scottish Government to i) provide national guidance, support, and professional learning for teachers in research-informed reading instruction, specifically systematic synthetic phonics; ii) ensure teacher training institutions train new teachers in research-informed reading instruction, specifically systematic synthetic phonics.

Scotland's literacy levels have been declining since 2006 due to a lack of research-informed resources and training for primary teachers. Scotland dropped from 6th to 23rd place in the OECD reading rankings in 15 years.

The struggle to raise standards in primary schools throughout England has had mixed results. Generally speaking, recognition of the importance of early instruction in the alphabetic code has been widespread, but a good deal of positive effect has been dampened by other, less beneficial trends, such as constructivist and inquiry-based teaching methods (see Glossary).

Vocal anti-phonics commentators and vested interests continue to mar progress towards literacy for all in the UK, but there are encouraging signs, such as the Phonics Screening Check and a greater acceptance of the fact that phonics is an important element in early primary teaching.

The Plowden Report 1967: It's not broken, so let's fix it

In 1967 in Britain, when Piaget's theories were at their peak of influence, a forcefully written paper called the Plowden Report was released. It heralded the first major shift towards 'child centred' teaching. This was not in response to declining literacy and numeracy. On the contrary, standards of both had been rising steadily since World War II.

Many of the recommendations were sensible and compassionate, such as the condemnation of corporal punishment and encouragement of contact with children's families. It even warned against an over-emphasis on play-based learning, saying, '[W]e certainly do not deny the value of learning "by description" or the need for practice of skills and consolidation of knowledge' (Blackstone 1976, 202).

However, this document became the perfect framework for progressive education. It created a false view that children needed to throw off the shackles of oppressive discipline and move to a more 'child centred' academic existence. Unfortunately, learning to read takes discipline. It takes practice and it takes a systematic, rigorous, direct instructional approach. 1960s Britain didn't want a bar of it.

The next two decades saw the dismantling of many of the structures that had brought widespread literacy success to millions of Britons. Standards started to decline.

The Education Reform Act 1988

By 1988, Margaret Thatcher's government decided that there needed to be an overhaul and through her Education Reform Act, several things happened that actually made the situation worse.

The *National Curriculum English Order* was introduced and in it, whole language, word-guessing and 'meaning-making' were emphasised. The influential Report of the National Curriculum English Working Group (DES 1989), known as the *Cox Report*, clearly stated that when learning to read, 'children should be encouraged to make informed guesses'.

By 1990, the National Curriculum had embedded the three-cueing system deeply within its standards documents. This was often referred to as the *Searchlight* model. Very little reference was made to phonics until May 1994, when *English in the National Curriculum: Draft Proposals* was released, and the pendulum began to swing back to more evidence-supported teaching methods.

The Office for Standards of Education (Ofsted) 1992

The moment the British government began to fund public schools, they also began to appoint inspectors of those schools to report to Parliament that the money was being well spent.

This began in 1833 with the secretary of the Privy Council education committee and grew from there. Unfortunately, by 1992 the system of inspectorates had become something of a raggle-taggle, vastly varied, decentralised apparatus. Prime Minister John Major oversaw the establishment of Ofsted through the Education (Schools) Act that year, as an attempt to bring it all back together under one administrative banner. Sir Jim Rose was appointed head of Ofsted in 1994 and held that position until 1999.

The National Literacy Strategy
Framework for Teaching 1998

A decade after the Education Reform Act, some inroads towards higher quality literacy instruction had been made, with the new *Framework for Teaching*. It stated:

> *When students read familiar and predictable texts, they can easily become over-reliant on their knowledge of context and grammar. They may pay too little attention to how words sound and how they are spelt. But if students cannot decode individual words through their knowledge of sounds and spellings, they find it difficult to get at the meaning of more complex, less familiar texts.*
>
> (DFES 2001, 4)

The document contained good news and bad news, in that it still recommended 'sight recognition' of high frequency words and the Searchlight model continued to be acceptable.

The Rose Report 2006

This kind of thing went back and forth until the House of Commons Education and Skills Committee conducted an inquiry into teaching children to read, concluding in February 2005.

The report, written by Sir Jim Rose, was called the *Independent Review of the Teaching of Early Reading*, and became known as the *Rose Report*, which stated:

> *Despite uncertainties in research findings, the practice seen by the review shows that the systematic approach, which is generally understood as "synthetic" phonics, offers the vast majority of young children the best and most direct route to becoming skilled readers and writers.*
>
> (Rose 2005, 4)

Letters and Sounds Program released 2009

In an effort to persuade schools to take on a synthetic phonics approach to early reading instruction, the UK government commissioned and released *Letters and Sounds*. It was offered free of charge to schools and contained a clear scope and sequence, a training manual, assessment sheets and a DVD to guide teachers.

Its advice was mostly sage:

> ... attention should be focused on decoding rather than on the use of unreliable strategies such as looking at the illustrations, rereading the sentence, saying the first sounds and guessing what might fit. ... Children who routinely adopt alternative cues for reading unknown words, instead of learning to decode them, find themselves stranded when texts become more demanding and meanings less predictable.

Unfortunately, it became 'yet another' phonics program that schools could choose from and often needed to be supplemented, as it was, in effect, a detailed framework rather than a self-contained program.

Match-funded phonics 2011–13

From 2011–13, the UK government offered to pay up to £3,000 if a school matched this amount to buy named/listed phonics programs, sets of decodable books, phonics training and phonics games and activities.

The mistake was the 'phonics games and activities'. Some schools bought thousands of pounds worth of 'phonics bits and pieces' in place of a fully resourced phonics program. This happened because schools were, in effect, trying to add resources to the Letters and Sounds program.

The National Phonics Screening Check 2012

To ensure that schools were equipped to teach children to read and were doing their job effectively, the Department for Education introduced a quick, low-stakes screening check for all children at the end of Year/Grade 1 and again at the end of Year/Grade 2 for all children who did not pass the first one.

The howls from those opposed to phonics were astonishing. The head of the National Union of Teachers went on the BBC and actually said, with a straight face, 'Children develop at different levels, the slow reader at five can easily be the good reader by the age of 11' (Harrison 2013). There is hardly a more stable and reliable predictor of reading success or failure than reading ability at age six.

Australia has since taken heed and proposed a similar check, again to bewildering opposition.

Out of all the English-speaking nations, England is the furthest ahead in terms of reading reform. All schools in England are mandated to use systematic synthetic phonics for early literacy instruction and the leading phonics programs are well written and robust.

In the Progress in International Reading Literacy Study (PIRLS), England has risen steadily since 2006 and outranked the US, Canada and Australia in 2016 (Mullis et al. 2017).

Sir Jim Rose and his cohorts continue to fight for excellent reading instruction in the UK. Many more are taking up the cause. Chapter 14 seeks to elaborate on the work of those who have received the baton.

References

Blackstone, T. (1967). The Plowden Report. *The British Journal of Sociology*, 18, 291–302. doi:10.2307/588641

Department for Education and Skills (DFES) Standards and Effectiveness Unit. (2001). *The National Literacy Strategy: Framework for Teaching* (3rd ed.). London: Author.

DES. (1989). English for Ages 5 to 16 (The Cox Report.) London: DES and Welsh Office.

Glennie, A. (2017). Petition to The Scottish Parliament for Improving Literacy Standards in Schools through Research-Informed Reading Instruction, 9 August.

Harrison, A. (2013). Phonics Test: More Than Two-Thirds of Children Pass New Phonics Test. *BBC News*. https://www.bbc.com/news/education-24381989

Mullis, I. V. S., Martin, M. O., Foy, P., & Hooper, M. (2017). *PIRLS 2016 International Results in Reading*. Boston College, TIMSS & PIRLS International Study Center. https://timssandpirls.bc.edu/pirls2016/index.html

Rose, J. (2005). *Independent Review of the Teaching of Early Reading*. London: Dept. for Education and Skills.

CHAPTER 13

The Land of Oz

Does your approach take more time to induce than an alternative that is equally effective? If so, the alternative wins. Does your approach address the full range of things children have to learn that any other approach covers? If not, the alternative wins. So teach it in less time, with provisions for the full range of students and content, and you win. Period. Step very far outside this box and you're wandering where you should not be: in the Land of Oz.

Siegfried Engelmann

Australia's educational history is somewhat different again from its UK and US cousins, yet it too continues to be prone to poor ideas and fads. Australia has a large indigenous population, which has both presented problems for education and demonstrated some remarkable solutions.

Indigenous Australians constitute less than 3% of the nation's population, and there are over 120 indigenous Australian languages in the country. These languages are often the first language of indigenous children entering school.

High rates of poverty and other adverse conditions place Aboriginal school-children at a hefty disadvantage. Yet despite what could be viewed as insurmountable barriers to literacy, large swathes of indigenous children are being successfully taught to read and write in regions of the country's Northern Territory (NT), Queensland and Western Australia. The NT, home to around 30% of the total Aboriginal population, has the largest concentration of indigenous Australians.

Aboriginal lawyer and activist Noel Pearson has been a key figure in getting Direct Instruction in literacy into schools, thus improving the educational landscape for indigenous children in the remote northern regions. Direct Instruction involves systematic, structured and scripted lessons, carefully sequenced and containing effective checks and balances to make sure no child is advanced to a higher skill level without gaining mastery of the preceding one. In 2015, 3,244 children from kindergarten to high school in these regions were assessed and only 8% of them could read and write above a Year 2 level. Two years later, about a third were now at their appropriate age level or above.

Yet critics wrung their hands about how Direct Instruction 'kills creativity'. Pearson soberly reminded them to put their romantic notions away. In an article in *The Australian* newspaper in October 2017, he wrote:

> *You give these kids a chance to read, you give them justice. And, if you're concerned about justice for Aboriginal children or remote and disadvantaged children generally, then the first duty of social justice we owe to them is a basic strong education.*

Deeply entrenched whole language culture

Australia's proximity to New Zealand, the birthplace of Reading Recovery, has also created something of a bias towards whole language and 'balanced literacy'.

Most teacher training institutes in the country promote whole language and equip their graduate teachers with very poor tools for literacy teaching.

Despite its poor evidence base, whole language techniques and culture pervade Australian education. From unions, whose leaders passionately oppose phonics, to the commercially produced 'reading diaries', unquestioningly bought and taken home, Australian schools are steeped in outdated practice.

National Inquiry into the Teaching of Literacy

In 2004, a team of 26 Australian reading scientists wrote a strong letter to the Minister for Education, Science and Training. It stated:

> *As researchers, psychologists, linguists and educators who have studied the processes underlying the development of reading, and who are familiar with the scientific research literature relating to the acquisition of reading, we are writing to you to express our concerns with the way in which reading is typically being taught in Australian schools.*
>
> (Open letter)

The experts warned that the whole language, whole word and 'balanced literacy' methods, popular throughout teacher training institutions and schools, were doing a great disservice to many children.

In response, the Australian government held an inquiry. The inquiry's aims were to investigate the quality of:

- the teaching of reading in Australian schools
- the assessment of reading proficiency, including identification of students with reading difficulties
- teacher training and the extent to which it prepares teachers for reading instruction

It concluded:

> The evidence is clear, whether from research, good practice observed in schools, advice from submissions to the Inquiry, consultations, or from Committee members' own individual experiences, that direct systematic instruction in phonics during the early years of schooling is an essential foundation for teaching children to read. Findings from the research evidence indicate that all students learn best when teachers adopt an integrated approach to reading that explicitly teaches phonemic awareness, phonics, fluency, vocabulary knowledge and comprehension. This approach, coupled with effective support from the child's home, is critical to success.

But looking into the problem and making recommendations is only as useful as the extent to which those recommendations are implemented.

The Dyslexia Working Party

In 2009, a subsequent inquiry by the Dyslexia Working Party made similar recommendations to the Parliamentary Secretary, focusing on obtaining a better deal for people affected by dyslexia. Parts of those recommendations were agreed to, but still not much trickled down to real practice at the coalface.

In a reprise of the 2004 letter that prompted the national inquiry in the first place, a group of now 36 eminent researchers again wrote to federal, state and territory education ministers in 2012. They said:

> Indeed, if the recommendations of the NITL (National Inquiry into the Teaching of Literacy) were adopted, wholesale retraining of teachers would be necessary to provide them with the understanding of literacy not presented to them in their own teacher training. We need a vast shake-up at all levels of teacher training. We ... urge your immediate attention to what has become a national disgrace.
>
> (Open letter)

Nearly another decade passed. Australia, and indeed all the countries in the English-speaking world, have all the information they need to ensure literacy for everyone. Yet nothing has really changed. Fad after fad continues to wash up on Australia's shores to be embraced by those who really ought to know better, while the 'long tail of underachievement' grows.

The positives in the Australian scene are encouraging, though. Despite an educational culture that is steeped in progressiveness and whole language, there are several grassroots and professional organisations made up of steely, no-nonsense people with their sleeves rolled up. The following chapter mentions a few of them.

Reference

Balogh, S. (2017). Noel Pearson says literacy teaching at heart of social justice. *The Australian*. https://www.theaustralian.com.au/news/nation/noel-pearson-says-literacy-teaching-at-heart-of-social-justice/news-story/6832bc75193fadda4aca5ca3ef545791

CHAPTER 14

The current scene

National inquiries into the teaching of reading have often come up with useful recommendations, but implementation has been slow. One of the factors in the ineffectiveness of inquiry recommendations is active opposition.

To counter the spread of misinformation, several individuals and organisations have set up hubs of knowledge, including blog sites, electronic mailing lists (listservs), Facebook pages and web pages.

This chapter introduces some of them in an effort to encourage the reader to become informed and active. There are also some recommendations regarding who to follow on Twitter, for insightful commentary on reading instruction and the greater subject of education in general.

Non-profit organisations

AUSPELD

History: Founded in 1968 by kindergarten teacher Yvonne Stewart as SPEcific Learning Difficulties.

Details: The group started in Sydney but soon had a branch in every state and were renamed AUSPELD. Their mission is to make themselves redundant one day by providing evidence-based information and advocacy on learning difficulties for parents, schools and governments.

'The main purpose of this national body would be to keep contact with the Commonwealth Government and to speak with one voice to Commonwealth politicians.'

Australian Dyslexia Association

History: Founded in 2007 by Jodi Clements.

Details: One of the first and most effective advocacy groups for people with dyslexia in Australia. They have spearheaded the campaign to have 'direct, explicit, systematic and multisensory teaching approaches for individuals with dyslexia or a related difference' throughout the nation.

British Dyslexia Association

History: Founded in 1972.
Details: The BDA is a lobby group, training organisation and information provider for people in the UK affected by dyslexia. They support regional development of other dyslexia associations. They also deal with cases of dyscalculia (problems with mathematics).

'The BDA has three campaign areas:

1. To encourage schools to work towards becoming dyslexia-friendly.
2. To reduce the number of dyslexic young people in the criminal justice system.
3. To enable dyslexic people to achieve their potential in the workplace.'

Children of the Code

History: Founded in 2003 by David Boulton.
Details: The Children of the Code website has a list of interviews with leading scientists, practitioners and commentators in the field of education. It is a fascinating repository of views from many sides of the great debate and well worth browsing.

'Statistically, more American children suffer long-term life-harm from the process of learning to read than from parental abuse, accidents, and all other childhood diseases and disorders combined. In purely economic terms, reading-related difficulties cost our nation more than the war on terrorism, crime, and drugs combined'.

CodeRead Dyslexia Network

History: Founded in 2018 by Dyslexia Support Australia administrators.
Details: This non-profit organisation was founded 'to create change and bring greater awareness of dyslexia to schools and the community. We will continue to support families & individuals with dyslexia, as well as act as an

official voice for parents with government & educators to improve education outcomes for those with dyslexia'.

Developmental Disorders of Language and Literacy Network (DDOLL)

History: 'The DDOLL network was established in 2003 with funding from the Australian Research Council. The group consists of scientists, clinicians, teachers and parents interested in discussing, and disseminating information about the investigation and treatment of developmental disorders of language and literacy through sound scientific methodology and evidence-based research. In order to maintain this focus, membership of the network is through invitation only'.

Comments: Though founded in Australia, the DDOLL Network has members from across the globe and actively engages in fascinating debate about the education scene as it pertains to literacy and literacy instruction. It is a goldmine of information and a must for anyone working in this field. Those who wish to join can contact the network by email.

Dyslexia Support Facebook pages

No matter where you live, suspicion of dyslexia or a dyslexia diagnosis can lead parents and teachers into a minefield. There are dozens of dyslexia support pages on Facebook, but only a handful are committed to providing evidence-based support. The rest have no qualms about posting and reposting harmful dyslexia myths, paying for members to inflate their status and selling time- and money-wasting resources.

If a no-nonsense, factual support page is what you require, then look no further than Dyslexia Support Australia (DSA). Even if you live outside Australia, their fact files alone provide answers to help people all over the world avoid the pitfalls.

They have been instrumental in helping to establish high quality regional support pages throughout Australia and are a model of how a grassroots movement can effect real change.

Five from Five

History: Founded in 2016 by Dr Jennifer Buckingham, Centre for Independent Studies, Australia.

Details: This non-profit initiative strives to provide free, accessible information for parents and teachers on best practice literacy instruction.

Their name comes from their understanding that children are most likely to achieve reading success if skilfully and explicitly taught the five keys to reading from the age of five.

'Five From Five is an initiative of the Centre for Independent Studies that aims to improve literacy levels by ensuring all children receive effective, evidence based reading instruction. Five From Five brings together an alliance of philanthropic organisations and individuals, researchers, educators, parents and professional associations'.

The International Dyslexia Association (IDA)

History: Formally organised in 1949 (after beginning in 1920) and known as the Orton Society, after Dr Samuel T. Orton and his pioneering work in the field.

Details: This is the oldest advocacy organisation for learning difficulties in the world. It has branches and roots across the globe and strives, very successfully, to bring together researchers, practitioners, legislators and parent movements in the quest to benefit those with dyslexia.

'To create a future for all individuals who struggle with dyslexia and other related reading differences so that they may have richer, more robust lives and access to the tools and resources they need'.

The International Foundation for Effective Reading Instruction (IFERI)

History: Founded in 2014, IFERI lists 15 committee members – but I happen to know that the glue sticking all of these parts together is the inspirational, tireless Debbie Hepplewhite from Phonics International.

Details: IFERI is intended to be a hub of information regarding research-based literacy instruction. It has guest bloggers and numerous forums, discussing everything from getting Ghana reading to synthetic phonics success stories and projects around the world.

'The aim of the International Foundation for Effective Reading Instruction is to contribute to raising standards of literacy in the English language based on robust research and high quality instruction in the teaching of reading, spelling and writing.

Our focus is on literacy for learners of all ages wherever in the world English is taught – regardless of whether English is the first or additional language'.

Learning Difficulties Australia (LDA)

History: Established in 1965 as the Diagnostic and Remedial Teachers' Association of Victoria, this group has a long history and occupies one of the most esteemed places in Australian education. It has an absorbing six part history, which can be found on its website.

Details: If you are in Australia and you have a question about teaching, literacy, language or assessment, this is an ideal place to start. They also publish, through Taylor and Francis, the *Australian Journal of Learning Disabilities (AJLD)*. LDA is, in fact, a rather terrific place to start no matter where you are.

'Learning Difficulties Australia is an association of teachers and other professionals dedicated to assisting students with learning difficulties through effective teaching practices based on scientific research, both in the classroom and through individualised instruction'.

MUSEC Briefings

History: Academics at the Macquarie University Special Education Centre (MUSEC) decided to offer, as a public service, a series of free, downloadable, one page documents about how reliable the evidence base for certain high profile interventions and practices is.

Details: Numbering 40 in total, these brilliantly written guides help parents and teachers know, at a glance, whether or not to pursue a certain course. They include positive as well as negative reviews and recommendations.

Funding for the MUSEC Briefings eventually dwindled, but all the documents can be found online with a simple Google search. Well worth looking into.

National Center for Learning Disabilities (NCLD)

History: Established by activists Carrie and Peter Rozelle in 1977 in response to the 'hurricane' that their undiagnosed learning disabled son Jack wrought on their family.

Details: This American organisation provides advice and resources to parents and legislators regarding best practice early literacy instruction and remediation.

'The mission of NCLD is to improve the lives of the 1 in 5 children and adults nationwide with learning and attention issues—by empowering parents and young adults, transforming schools and advocating for equal rights and opportunities. We're working to create a society in which every individual possesses the academic, social and emotional skills needed to succeed in school, at work and in life'.

National Center on Response to Intervention

History: Founded in 2007 with a grant from the US Office of Special Education Programs and continued by the American Institutes of Research.

Details: This organisation provides support for states, districts and schools implementing Response to Intervention and Multi-Tiered System of Support for both academic needs and behaviour of school students.

'The services provided by our staff are designed to assist states, districts, and schools to successfully implement and scale-up MTSS/RTI [Multi-Tier System of Supports/Response to Intervention] and its components. To determine what services may be needed, staff collaboratively problem-solve with the requesting state, district, or school to (a) identify and prioritize the areas of need, and (b) select evidence-based practices that can best meet those needs'.

National Institute for Direct Instruction (NIFDI)

History: Created in 1997 to support the implementation of Direct Instruction worldwide.

Details: Direct Instruction, its many programs and its history could be the subject of a book in its own right. Project Follow Through, the most extensive educational experiment ever conducted, concluded that 'no other program had the results that approached the positive impact of Direct Instruction' (Meyer 1984). Suffice to say that this site is a perfect starting point for teachers and school leaders to understand the potential impact Direct Instruction could have on education.

'Direct Instruction operates on five key philosophical principles:

- All children can be taught.
- All children can improve academically and in terms of self-image.
- All teachers can succeed if provided with adequate training and materials.
- Low performers and disadvantaged learners must be taught at a faster rate than typically occurs if they are to catch up to their higher-performing peers.

- All details of instruction must be controlled to minimize the chance of students' misinterpreting the information being taught and to maximize the reinforcing effect of instruction'.

National Right to Read Foundation (NRRF)

History: Founded by Robert Sweet and Jim Jacobson in 1993 to educate the public about evidence-based literacy instruction.

Details: This website provides a wealth of resources, including published research, studies, articles and links for parents and educators who wish to improve literacy instruction.

'The truth about reading English:

- The *myths* say reading is confusing ... the truth is reading is logical.
- The *myths* say reading is difficult ... the truth is reading is attainable.
- The *myths* say reading can only be taught well by experts ... the truth is anyone can teach reading.
- The *myths* say reading is not accessible to those with special needs ... the truth is anyone can learn to read.'

PBS Kids

History: The American Public Broadcasting Service (PBS) won a US Department of Education grant in 2005 to devise some TV shows to help children to read.

Details: The Ready to Learn grant has extended to encompass a website and TV shows that provide education in reading, mathematics, science, spelling and vocabulary.

The Reading League

History: Founded in 2015 by literacy Professor Maria Murray.

Details: This American advocacy body aims to provide practitioners in the field with the most up to date information regarding teaching reading. Their aim is to spread evidence-based practice as far and wide as possible by having regular meetings with various stakeholders and increasing awareness through conferences and publications.

Their website lists a host of advocacy organisations and partners worldwide who share their mission.

'There is a lot that can be done to help each child and adult in need of learning how to read. There is a lot that can be done to help each educator learn what evidence we have for various skills and strategies. We can help'.

Reading Reform Foundation (UK)

History: Founded in 1989 by a group of educators and researchers to help stem the tide of illiteracy worldwide by promoting alphabetic code based teaching.

Details: The Foundation works to disseminate best practice information to parents, teachers and government departments. Apart from a rich website with free resources and articles, the members of the foundation actively campaign for reading reform. As a result of their campaigning, all local-authority-maintained schools have been mandated to use synthetic phonics in early literacy teaching since 2014.

'For too long now the teaching of reading has been affected by the idea that children should learn by discovery and "incidental" phonics teaching, leading to the rejection of systematic, explicit phonics instruction. This idea is deeply ingrained in education and still has a powerful influence on how reading is taught, despite having no scientific validity'.

Society for the Scientific Study of Reading

History: Founded in 1993 by professor of psychology Ron Carver.

Details: The SSSR sponsors conferences and a scientific journal about reading, language and literacy called *Scientific Studies of Reading*.

'The circle of going from fad to fad in reading will never be broken unless reading researchers demand that unusual theoretical claims are backed up with unusually sound empirical evidence'.

ResearchEd

History: Founded in 2013 by Tom Bennett with assistance from Helene O'Shea.

Details: What started as a one-off grassroots conference on research in education has now become a worldwide phenomenon. ResearchEd events are held throughout the year all over Britain, in Canada, Australia, New Zealand and parts of Europe.

They are low-cost conferences, with speakers and venues donating their space and time so that teachers and other educators can come together easily, bust myths, share findings and move toward a more evidence-informed educational landscape.

Their stated mission has six key points:

- 'raise research literacy
- bring people together
- promote collaboration
- increase awareness
- promote research
- explore what works'

SPELL-Talk

History: Launched in 2006 by speech-language pathologist Dr Jan Wasowicz from Learning by Design Inc.

Details: Learning by Design Inc. is the parent company to a range of programs and products for literacy known as SPELL-Links. As a public service, the company established a listserv called SPELL-Talk. This dynamic discussion forum connects educators and researchers from around the globe.

Commercial organisations that engage in activism

There are many reputable literacy resource providers in the world. Mentioning them all would be quite daunting. Instead, this section gives a snapshot of some outstanding for-profit organisations that also engage in activism. They provide free resources and advice. They speak out in the media and make submissions to government about best practice. They do this with consistency and sincerity; not as convenient sound-bites or cynical power-grabs, but over and above selling their brand.

The Learning Zoo

Founded by consultant and activist Anne Glennie, with the mission of teaching every child in Scotland to read. Anne writes books, programs and blogs to help raise awareness of best practice in teaching reading.

MultiLit

This organiation was founded in 1995 by Kevin and Robyn Wheldall as part of a research initiative at Macquarie University in Sydney, Australia. From their very beginnings, much of their work was focused on helping disadvantaged and indigenous students.

Three major non-profit initiatives have sprung from there:

1. MUSEC Briefings – see above.
2. The DDOLL Network – see above.
3. Nomanis – a free journal published and funded by MultiLit Pty Ltd which is 'a vehicle for promoting the ideas and evidence about effective instruction in reading and related skills, for teachers, parents, fellow professionals and policy makers'.

Phonics International

The indefatigable Debbie Hepplewhite finds time in between writing high quality, low cost online systematic synthetic phonics programs (many parts of which are free to view and download) to be a government lobbyist extraordinaire.

Debbie writes articles, advises government and is the founder of several literacy initiatives (UK RRF and IFERI, listed above).

Spelfabet

Speech pathologist Alison Clarke does much more than provide a high quality suite of resources to teach the big six of literacy.

Her extremely impressive free videos show effective techniques for teaching reading and spelling. Her blog successfully bridges the gap between research and practice and gives up to date answers to so many of the current tricky questions in the field.

Thinking Reading

Founded in 2011 by Dianne and James Murphy, Thinking Reading was set up to educate about effective practice in the secondary sector.

Thinking Reading challenges government policy and works with like-minded organisations to bring about better quality reading instruction in the UK.

Bloggers/tweeters/activists

Resistance to tweets and blogs is futile! If you aren't already on Twitter or if you haven't signed up for anyone's blog, but you enjoy debate and information on education and literacy, here are some tweeters who also blog that may be a great starting point:

- Greg Ashman: Filling the Pail
- Alison Clarke: Spelfabet
- Belinda Dekker: Dekker Delves into Dyslexia blog
- David Didau: Learning Spy
- Carl Hendrick: Chronotope blog
- John Kenny: John Kenny Blog
- Mike Lloyd Jones: The Phonics Blog
- Doug Lemov: Field Notes
- Andrew Old: Teaching Battleground
- Michael Salter: Pocket Quintilian
- Tim Shanahan: Shanahan on Literacy
- Pamela Snow: The Snow Report
- John Walker: The Literacy Blog
- Kevin Wheldall: Notes from Harefield

Reference

Meyer, L. A. (1984). Long-Term Academic Effects of the Direct Instruction Project Follow Through. *The Elementary School Journal*, 84(4), 380–94. doi:10.1086/461371

CHAPTER 15

Why changing your mind is good for you

It is the nature of every person to err, but only the fool perseveres in error.

Marcus Tullius Cicero

The vast majority of children can learn to read and write. It is a primary school's job to ensure that this happens. And yet, many children enter and leave high school illiterate.

A teaching career provides opportunities to grow professionally. It is a career with lifelong learning at its heart. Some teachers are fortunate enough to have excellent training and mentoring from the start, whilst others are disadvantaged by being equipped with poor tools.

Some educators are prepared to make the necessary changes in their own practice to keep up with research. Others have no urge to do this, and still others actively oppose it.

This chapter brings together some of my experiences with teachers. In arguments about teaching reading, my colleagues and I have often been accused of teacher-bashing. Nothing could be further from the truth.

Sometimes teachers simply get bad tools to work with. Sometimes they get false information. What they do when they realise this can be described using three broad teacher types.

Type 1: The Lifelong Learner

I was once approached by a very smart, very nice teacher who wanted to strike out on her own and get into specialist reading tutoring. She asked if I would train and employ her after she attended one of my workshops.

Angela was a fully trained Reading Recovery teacher. I was still fairly unfamiliar with Reading Recovery, so my first task was to observe her techniques and see how she could fit into the practice.

She demonstrated the three-cueing system, whereby children were instructed to get words off the page by looking at pictures, guessing words from context or from the initial couple of letters. I simply couldn't see the point. So I offered training in phonemic awareness and phonics instead.

She stopped using whole language and developed her skills in systematic, explicit, structured literacy teaching. She became a highly sought-after, effective practitioner.

Angela was reluctant at first to stop using the hard-won skills that Reading Recovery had taught her, but being a Lifelong Learner, she let them go and started using her time more effectively.

Angela had the intelligence to evaluate her performance and the flexibility to discard ineffective ideas. The power of dogma in her training was overcome by her ability to observe her techniques and her lack of arrogance helped her to feel comfortable with radical change.

Those who seek and implement best practice and adjust their techniques accordingly are the ones who stand to make the biggest difference in children's lives. This, of course, can be an extremely uncomfortable experience, especially for educators who have been using lower quality instructional methods for many years. The guilt of having helped fewer children can be overwhelming. This is why teachers need to demand the highest quality training and resources right from the start.

Type 2: The Blissful Plodder

Teachers at the beginning of their careers still have much to learn. Studying for three or four years and then being launched into a classroom and expected to teach 20+ tiny individuals is a task I do not envy. Some relish the thought of growing and learning with their career; others, not so much.

The Blissful Plodder is a teacher who knows about as much at the end of his or her career as at the beginning.

I've met many plodders at various stages of their teaching journey but most of them occupy the beginning and end sections – the young ones tending to leave teaching around the middle because of the demands of the job.

Those who do survive are often kind, caring people who like to work with children, but still have very little idea of up to date teaching practice in one or more areas. They are the ones treading water until retirement. It's very hard to get cross with such people and often they have redeeming qualities of compassion, humour and gentleness that allow parents and leaders to overlook their shortcomings.

I am reminded of a school principal I once knew. His small rural school had a reputation for excellence in mathematics and science as well as a strong foundation of fair and equitable discipline. He was an elderly, affable man, larger than life, and took great pride in knowing the names of all the students and their parents. He really was charming and obviously loved his role and was loved equally by those around him.

The school's literacy teaching and support, however, were failing many of the students. All teachers were trained in analytic phonics and the reading intervention program was a mishmash of whole language techniques.

I once asked him if he would consider updating his literacy teaching and intervention to be more in line with current findings on the subject. He laughed and told me he 'didn't give a fig' for current findings. Reading science was not of any interest whatsoever. And so, his lowest-performing students were consigned to ineffective intervention, and those whose families could afford it sought external tutoring.

Blissful Plodders are not bad people, but their effect can be disastrous. Blissful plodders are hard to disagree with, because they don't hold any strong opinions about very much at all, but they are still resistant to change.

Type 3: The Rigid Idealist

Rigid Idealists are those who remain inflexible in their opinions despite evidence to the contrary and who stick doggedly to what they initially thought was correct.

If they manage to create an empire whilst doing so, that's very bad news for children. Take the case of Marie Clay, author of the Reading Recovery program, a worldwide education phenomenon. Since its inception in New Zealand in 1983, it has spread to thousands of schools, dozens of education departments and hundreds of school districts across America, Canada, Australia and Europe.

The teacher training involves total immersion in Reading Recovery culture and lasts over a year. It involves theory, practice and rigorous observation and critique from behind two-way mirrors.

It is systematic and extremely effective in maintaining program fidelity; that is, teachers are strongly discouraged from veering off the prescribed program.

The setup is quite remarkable. The only problem is: it's wrong. It doesn't work nearly as effectively as structured literacy. In fact, it can sometimes make things worse for students.

But back to rigid idealism. Marie Clay was nothing if not charismatic and forceful. She had a certain idea about teaching reading to struggling readers and nothing was going to make her change her mind.

Robert Sweet gives probably the best example of a Rigid Idealist and the catastrophic consequences of such inflexibility. Robert was heavily involved in drafting US legislation to help improve how reading was taught in schools.

Top researchers worked on the definition of scientifically based reading research and concluded that funding would be provided for the implementation of programs that were based on science and included the five essential components of reading instruction.

Robert writes:

As you can imagine, with six billion in funding for Reading First there were 'lobbyists' who descended on me, one of whom was Dame Marie Clay and her entourage. They had a major center for Reading Recovery in Ohio and she brought her top staff in to meet with me in the Rayburn House Office Building. I think there were five of her staff and the 'lady' herself, Dame Marie Clay.

We were in a small conference room and I was the only staffer who met them. Their purpose was to lobby me to change the requirements of the draft legislation to accommodate Reading Recovery. I listened to their presentation, and then expressed my concern that the content of Reading Recovery was weak on any decoding training, and was in effect, a whole language program.

They were taken aback but I told Dame Marie Clay that she has a wonderful opportunity to modify her program, and to include the proper training in decoding skills for teachers who were spending a year in training at the facility in Ohio. I told her that she could help to turn the tide towards reading science that had been confirmed by two major reports that had just been issued.

I told her that Reading Recovery did NOT meet the requirements of the new legislation and that unless they changed the program, it would not be funded.

At that point, Dame Clay looked at me with steely eyes and said: 'We will not change a thing in our program. But, we will modify our description of Reading Recovery to comply with the law.' To which I retorted, 'I think that is one of the most despicable things anyone has ever said to me.' Needless to say, she was not pleased with my declaration and the meeting ended without any agreement.

President Bush signed the Reading First bill into law on January 8, 2002. Unfortunately, the implementation of the law was not faithfully carried out, and I am sure that Reading Recovery was funded ... and that is why the What Works Clearinghouse later touted Reading Recovery as a 'research based' reading program.

(Personal communication)

This is where philosophy creeps into education and where the real damage occurs. Marie Clay had the power to alter her program and speak up for systematic synthetic phonics. She could have changed the lives of countless children for the better if she had accepted the fact that her program needed to change.

She was not unintelligent or incapable of altering Reading Recovery, but she made it very clear to all who encountered her that it was 'my way or the highway'.

The hard questions

My colleagues and I are supporters and practitioners of structured, explicit, systematic literacy instruction, with phonological awareness and phonics as a starting point. Collectively, we have worked for hundreds of thousands of hours with countless children.

I don't think it would be untrue if I were to state that if we were presented with convincing evidence that something other than what we are doing right now is better for children, we would, one and all, gladly admit that we were wrong and would, without hesitation, embrace the new method.

So what kind of teacher are you?

What kind of teacher is your child's teacher?

It's time to demand and supply higher quality literacy instruction for everyone. It's time that teachers overcame the limitations of their training, their school environment or the education system itself and challenged plodders and idealists.

CHAPTER 16

Cults and catchphrases

Why do bad ideas persist in education? What makes fads so attractive and why aren't we better at avoiding garbage?

One of the factors is charisma. Likeable people are easy to believe. Confident people are easy to follow.

On a large scale, the power of personality can lead to extraordinary circumstances. In education, marketing often trumps merit when schools and districts buy into products and personalities regardless of substance.

Some educators command a cult-like following. I see it all the time. Some education companies remain relatively small, whilst others become large, influential worldwide enterprises. The cult-like ones usually have some or all of the attributes below:

1. **Charismatic leader**

   Cults are founded on their gurus. Blind devotion to one person who can do no wrong is a dangerous thing.

   In education, ask yourself, how personality-heavy is the company's promotion and marketing material? I think I may have seen one picture of Romalda Spalding or Samuel Orton in my entire career. Instead, their ideas and programs speak for themselves. There are other companies whose stock in trade is their leader.

2. **New coinages**

   Cults often have language exclusive to the cult. This serves to keep the external world out and to bond members together.

   In education, this includes rituals and language that the mainstream doesn't use or that you won't see in any peer-reviewed research papers. There is nothing wrong with a brand carving out its unique spot in the marketplace, but I start to worry when companies invent in-house terms for phenomena in reading that either don't exist or haven't been named and agreed upon by consensus.

The three-cueing system is a perfect example of a coinage gone crazy. No one can trace its source, and it has no experimental data to support it, yet it is repeated, adopted and defended the world over (Adams 1998).

New coinages can quickly become vehicles for disease-mongering if not kept in check. 'Scotopic sensitivity syndrome', 'brain buttons' and 'barking at print' are not actual things. See Chapter 19 for more on this.

3. **Isolation of trainees**

   Continuing to belong to a cult relies upon having no opposing views or reasons to question the cult. Families and colleagues are often portrayed as dangerous to cult members, who are slowly brainwashed to reject their closest kin in favour of the cult.

   In several instances, I have observed that trainees of certain programs are guided to think they are somewhat *special* and more important than their ordinary colleagues. They are also trained not to look elsewhere for other tools, but to look within the programs and 'research' of one particular company only.

   When working with children who have developmental language disorders, the most effective practitioners are effective precisely because they can draw on a rich background of experience and training from a wide range of sources. Beware a practitioner who calls themselves a [insert brand-name here] teacher. If all you have is a hammer, everything looks like a nail.

4. **Dissemination**

   To survive and continue making money, cults need to constantly gather new members. This often becomes the sole activity of devotees.

   I was once asked to go on a live radio talkback show to discuss dyslexia. My role was to define the condition and talk about possible avenues for parents whose children were struggling with reading. During the segment, which consisted of taking calls from the public, one woman came on the phone and started talking about one particular reading program that she had been trained in.

   It was as if she was reading from a flyer, the way she was describing it. There was no acknowledgement that this was a general discussion or that there were several brands that offered a good approach to dyslexia; it was simply all about the brand *she'd* been trained in. We ended the call as quickly and politely as possible, but it was such terrible form. She was acting like a brainwashed fool. Nothing puts me off a brand quicker than this kind of behaviour.

5. **Cognitive dissonance**

   In cults, devotees often have to decide between two opposing views, both of which seem factual. For example:

   - 'The leader is a kind and benevolent person … yet I have witnessed or been subjected to cruelty by this person'.

- 'The teachings of this group recommend rejection of material possessions, yet the higher-ups in the group live in luxury'.

The discomfort that arises when a person becomes aware of two opposing views that seem factual is called cognitive dissonance. Some people try to relieve that discomfort by fabricating a non-truthful justification for the dissonance:

- 'The leader *is* kind and benevolent. His cruelty is an act of correction with loving intent'.
- 'The higher-ups only live in luxury to present a successful picture to the outside world'.

In education, some teachers are uncomfortable to find that intensive intervention with a certain program or method still results in a need for ongoing support. Yet they remain convinced that what they are using is the 'best program available', so failure, therefore, must be the fault of the child, the child's family, the teachers before or after the intervention, or society itself.

Teachers who accept cognitive dissonance as part and parcel of their repertoire are not to be trusted. There are several programs that train their teachers to expect a 20% failure rate. The ones their teaching doesn't help are labelled and discontinued or referred elsewhere for 'special teaching'. This is unacceptable and not justifiable by saying it is the child who isn't right for the teaching. The teaching can and should be right for the child.

6. **Exclusive benefits**

   Cults usually make the leader(s) wealthy and influential but benefit few others.

   There is nothing wrong with making a living out of writing education programs. However, if you let your marketing, your personality, your trainees and/or your brand become more important than scientific consensus, you are in danger of forming a cult.

   There is plenty of room in the market for good quality resources. Those whose goal it is to pitch in and raise standards across the board do not tear down competing brands, but rather, work collaboratively with their colleagues for the greater good.

   As a current example, at the time of writing, there are several companies that publicly oppose any government-mandated phonics screening checks in schools. One theory is they fear that their brand will be shown to be inadequate by such screening. Throwing out positive initiatives like that is tantamount to throwing children under the bus. The moment you choose your brand and the benefits it bestows on you, over the common good, is the moment you start walking the cult path.

7. **No tolerance for critical inquiry**

Cults are known to routinely forbid devotees from viewing negative media reports about their leaders. Devotees are also punished for bringing into question any doubts or misgivings about the cult. Rather than engage in intelligent, open debate, cult leaders often refuse to speak in public or listen to opponents.

Social media has given us many advantages, not least in helping to spot cultish behaviour in groups and companies. It is a huge red flag when people delete and block those who question their stance on a certain point. Of course, there are certain boundaries of politeness that, if overstepped, warrant deleting and blocking, but silencing those who question, ask for sources of information or engage in debate are clear signs that marketing has trampled merit.

The oxbow lake effect

Marie Clay is not the only example of a leader in education caught up in her own glory. Being open to criticism is a necessary attribute of a researcher. Beware the author who does not allow scrutiny.

In geography, there is a phenomenon known as an oxbow lake. A river flows and as it does, it wears a path into the landscape. That flow is like the flow of information coursing through any field of human study. The greater the number of minds applied to the subject, the greater the amount of information and knowledge applies and the deeper and more certain the understanding within that field grows.

Sometimes, along the course of a river, obstacles are encountered and a portion of the water is diverted in a slightly different direction. This can take place in science by the discovery of new information. Scientists begin to look at the field in new ways and practitioners move towards an improved model. This new path made by a river is called a meander. Sometimes, the alternative path turns out to be an unworkable model, and the mainstream, through force of evidence, creates a new, straight channel in the direction it was originally going.

Meanders can become totally isolated when a new channel is formed and the resulting feature is known as an oxbow lake (the shape of the lake looks like an ox's collar, or bow) (Figure 16.1).

Similarly, in education, some authors begin with good intentions and their ideas and preferences can provide food for thought that take the field on new and interesting meanders. But sometimes their ideas begin to clash with the mainstream. Instead of working to continue flowing with the accumulated

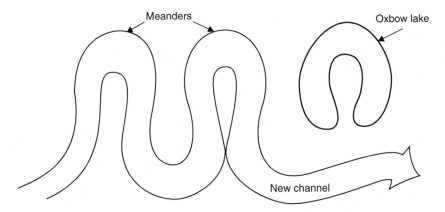

Figure 16.1 Oxbow lake

knowledge and best practice, they close themselves off from scrutiny and criticism, eventually cutting themselves off completely.

Oxbow lakes are prone to stagnation. Innovation, improvement, freshness and growth cannot take place in such an environment.

Reference

Adams, M. J. (1998). The Three-Cueing System. In F. Lehr and J. Osborn (Eds.), *Literacy for All: Issues in Teaching and Learning*, pp. 73–99. New York: Guilford Press.

CHAPTER 17

Won't get fooled again

Logical fallacy

I'm not a psychologist or a philosopher, and I don't pretend to have deep insight into the workings of the human mind. I do, however, have a fascination for patterns, whether they be cloud formations, spelling irregularities or the patterns of human behaviour when defending daft ideas.

In education, as in many fields, bad ideas can persist, and as a result, the vulnerable suffer. It fascinates me how people (including me) can accept and hold as fact things that are demonstrably untrue.

In this chapter, I am going to define and illustrate common examples of errors in thinking. I will illustrate these in a variety of ways:

- how I got fooled
- how someone else fooled others
- how this type of thinking is used in education to keep bad ideas alive, well and making cash

In this and the next chapter, we will look at two types of thinking that support irrational decisions:

- logical fallacy: arguments used to persuade others, but that, when taken apart, don't actually make sense and shouldn't be considered as evidence of truth
- cognitive bias: things we believe that make us judge the truth of claims in illogical ways

Logical fallacy

First, a confession: In my life, I have been presented with all kinds of convincing-sounding nonsense, and as a result I have been persuaded to believe what has turned out to be, in fact, rubbish. To list them here would take up a whole book in itself. Suffice to say, I have been very naive and deluded.

I've had to work hard to be less gullible. The hardest step was admitting I was wrong. But I can admit that, and I'll continue to admit it should I find myself in the wrong again. Nothing terrible has happened to me for taking that first step. In fact, changing my views and bending towards a more realistic perspective on life has been beneficial in many ways.

In the first few examples, I'm going to use a publicly available speech by a children's writer called Mem Fox. You can find the text of that speech by searching its title, *The Folly of Jolly Old Phonics*. I have used excerpts from it as a gold standard in logical fallacy and a typical representation of arguments thrown at my colleagues and me in the great debate.

This speech was presented in 2008 to a conference of school principals in New Zealand. Fox begins by alluding to educators in New Zealand being unimpressed with the results of the standards of literacy in their country. Rightly so: in 2008, 40% of New Zealand adults were reported as being functionally illiterate. That is, they couldn't read well enough to understand maps or prescription information or fill out basic forms, etc.

She then goes on to blame one of the pillars of literacy instruction, *phonics*, for this situation. Her speech also promotes whole language and reading *to* children as the solution, which is quite convenient if you write children's books. It's not so convenient if systematic, code-based instruction is what you need.

Ad hominem

Literally: *to the man* (Figure 17.1). This type of thinking is used in arguments when one side cannot think of a good enough reason to dispute another's claims, and so attacks their character instead.

How some try to fool others using ad hominem attacks

> *A modest man, who has much to be modest about*
>
> Winston Churchill on Clement Atlee

Figure 17.1 Ad hominem

> *He's like a shiver waiting for a spine.*
>
> Paul Keating on John Hewson

> *Filthy Story-Teller, Despot, Liar, Thief, Braggart, Buffoon, Usurper, Monster, Ignoramus Abe, Old Scoundrel, Perjurer, Robber, Swindler, Tyrant, Field-Butcher, Land-Pirate.*
>
> *Harper's Weekly* on Abraham Lincoln

Politics and ad hominem go hand in hand. Though politicians are supposed to be debating ideas, they are not above bringing their opponents' character into their arguments. Though there have been some admirable witticisms in politics, the ad hominem fallacy was taken to a new low in Donald Trump's 2016 presidential campaign. He attacked his main opponent, Hilary Clinton so viciously that he had crowds at his rallies chanting, 'Lock her up!' Rather than attack her party's policy, Trump accused her of being of poor character, a criminal and a liar. This is nothing new in politics and is certainly an effective strategy given Trump's election success.

How ad hominem is used in education

In her speech, Mem Fox mentions several programs, but particularly two evidence-based ones: Spalding and Jolly Phonics. She said, with irony:

> *... programs such as the Spalding Method ... and Jolly Phonics – by the very fact of their being so expensive and so well-marketed – must be better than anything you had before.*

Neither is particularly expensive and certainly both do not rely on the slick marketing of other, less research-supported programs. The success of Spalding and Jolly Phonics lies in the fact that they work well. It's really quite simple. Attacking the authors' character and motives is a cheap shot, and certainly doesn't disprove their methods.

Argumentum ad populum/bandwagon

Literally: *appeal to the people* (Figure 17.2). This is also called the bandwagon fallacy. It is an argument founded on the notion that something must be correct because so many people agree with it.

Figure 17.2 Argumentum ad populum/bandwagon

How I got fooled by the bandwagon fallacy

My 12 year old daughter once complained to me that the computer-based maths homework she had to do was pointless and repetitive and eating up too much of her free time. On close inspection, I could see what she meant. She was required to score an arbitrary 1,000 points doing much the same problem over and over again. There was very little sensitivity to the fact that she understood and could use the information in the problems and was ready for the next level.

When I mentioned this to her teacher, the response was, 'No one else has complained'. This caused me to accept that perhaps this boring, pointless program was good for my daughter after all.

What I should have said was, 'The fact that no one else has complained doesn't make it a good program'. Hindsight is a wonderful thing.

The good news is, my daughter proved immune to this fallacy, and continued to complain and was eventually allowed to drop the program altogether. Her maths has not suffered.

How some try to fool others with the bandwagon fallacy

Advertising: the home of twisted logic. How else would you be persuaded to switch your brand of cat food if, in tests, eight out of ten owners *didn't* say their cats preferred it?

Back in the days when smoking was good for you and advertising standards were nonexistent, companies like Lucky Strike would put interesting statistics into their campaign to persuade you buy their cigarettes: '20,679 physicians say Luckies are less irritating!' I love that precise number, as if it couldn't possibly be made up because, look, all the digits are *different*!

How the bandwagon fallacy is used in education

Take this baffling quote from Fox:

> *The current methods used to teach reading in the USA are causing such a worrying decline in reading standards that many American states have hired teachers from Australia and New Zealand who are working at this moment to improve literacy in failing schools. There are in 536 of these teachers in New York alone.*

I can only guess that Fox means 536 whole language–trained teachers. It sounds fairly impressive. That's a lot of teachers fighting the good fight. Except that when you break through this fallacy and look at the real story, it's not quite what you think.

At the start of the millennium, the New York Department of Education began to suffer a teacher shortage. Employment of teachers from overseas was one of the solutions to that shortage. Some of them came from Australia and New Zealand. Add to this the fact that New York employs about 75,000 teachers. This means that Fox's dream team makes up about 0.7% of the total teacher population. Quite a tiny bandwagon, really. More of a band-rollerskate.

But even if all the teachers *were* using the dubious methods championed by Fox, and even if their numbers were ten times the odd 536, it still wouldn't be evidence of the effectiveness of whole language.

Straw man

This is a way of arguing by changing or exaggerating an opponent's position so that it can be easily refuted (Figure 17.3). You make a man out of straw, attack and knock it down, stick pins in it and then claim victory.

How the straw man is used in education

The classic straw man from whole language proponents is the assertion that some people think phonics is the *only* component of effective literacy instruction. Fox says:

Figure 17.3 Straw man fallacy

So it's disappointing to discover that many parents, politicians and even a few principals think that decoding phonics correctly is indeed reading.

Nope. Reading is the ability to decode *and* comprehend print as outlined in the Simple View of Reading. Systematic, synthetic phonics is a starting point that will result in success for the greatest number of people. It is a necessary but not sufficient ingredient in the process of learning to read. Other ingredients are necessary too.

Snow and Juel sum up the importance of phonics beautifully in a chapter of the superlative *The Science of Reading: A Handbook* (2007):

... attention to small units in early reading instruction is helpful for all children, harmful for none, and crucial for some.

This is about as radical is it gets.

Who *are* these people who advocate phonics only? I've got a feeling they're all made of straw and living in Mem Fox's attic.

This ... therefore that

Or in Latin, *post hoc ergo propter hoc* (Figure 17.4). When two things happen around the same time, it does not mean that one caused the other, though it is often argued that this is the case. In summary: correlation isn't necessarily causation.

In his fascinating website and book *Spurious Correlations*, author and researcher Tyler Vigen shows some hilarious examples of matching data sets that have nothing to do with one another.

For example, Figure 17.5 shows how it would be easy to equate the number of people who ate margarine in the US with the number of people who got divorced in Maine from 2000 to 2009. If you believe the diagram, one seems to have caused the other.

The book shows correlations between all kinds of unrelated things, like per capita consumption of chicken and crude oil imports, but its deeper purpose

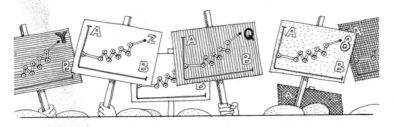

Figure 17.4 This ... therefore that

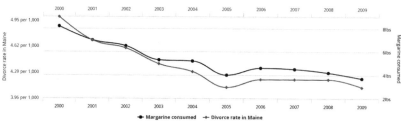

Figure 17.5 Correlation isn't necessarily causation: Divorce rate in Maine correlates to per-capita consumption of margarine (US). Adapted from Vigen, *Spurious Correlations* (2015)

is to show that while some things are related (be it simply in quantity), they don't necessarily have a causal connection (Figure 17.5).

How post hoc ergo propter hoc *fooled me*

I learned to read very early. I'm quite lucky. My father used Glenn Doman's *Teach Your Baby to Read* flashcard system for my older siblings as a way of expanding their vocabulary and I insisted on joining in. I just happened to have the sort of brain that took to reading through very little exposure to a small set of words.

For many years I attributed my early literacy to the Doman method. My reasoning was:

My father did flashcards.
I learned to read.
Therefore, I can teach people to read doing flashcards.

It wasn't until I tried and failed with this method on two of my daughters that I realised that I actually learned to read because it was easy for me. The method was almost immaterial.

What was needed in the case of my dyslexic daughter was explicit teaching of the alphabetic code with lots of fluency practice. Fortunately, I was able to help her with that and she reads well now.

How post hoc ergo propter hoc *is used in education*

Reading to children can help them to read in a small number of cases. It is disastrous to apply this correlation to all children.

In her speech, Fox tells the story of a number of bright children who were lucky enough to not have dyslexia and who lived in a supportive, caring home environment.

All of them learned to read before entering school and Fox puts this down to the fact that their parents read them the same stories over and over again.

Indeed, some children with an aptitude for converting print to speech will be able to figure out the alphabetic code with a small, repetitive sample of the language, but many won't. These events correlate, but one doesn't cause the other.

It is logical to require that a system of early literacy instruction include children not endowed with that aptitude.

Appeal to authority

Something is true because an 'expert' said it was true (Figure 17.6). Experts can be three things: correct, wrong or not really experts. Ideas are either well-supported by research or they aren't, regardless of who is saying them.

This can also be used the other way round to claim that a person commenting on a subject is not suitably qualified and therefore their position must be wrong.

Teaching reading and writing is a perfect subject for scientific analysis. There are many different professions interested in and doing research on the subject. Researchers from various fields agree on a plausible, workable model of the process of learning to read. This is what is meant by a *settled* science.

If you make a claim about literacy, reading scientists won't take much notice if you can't provide some clear evidence. It doesn't matter who you are, whether you have a knighthood or how many letters you have after your name.

How appeal to authority fooled me

I once went to see an extremely charismatic speaker who wrote a book about the way the human brain can adapt. The book was full of stories about people

Figure 17.6 Appeal to authority

who overcame all types of brain-damaging illness and injury to make themselves functional again.

Norman Doidge and his *Brain That Changes Itself* bestseller was really appealing. Something of the halo effect (see Chapter 18) was at play in my acceptance of Doidge's theories, but also, he just had so many qualifications. According to his website, he is 'a psychiatrist, psychoanalyst, researcher, author, essayist and poet'. How could he be wrong?

I was enthralled by his stories of people who showed improvements in brain function through various repetitive techniques. His beautifully written book brought neuroscience to the layman but proved, unfortunately, that a little knowledge can be a dangerous thing.

Tucked in amongst the joyous anecdotes was a description of a maverick neuroscientist, Michael Merzenich, who had allegedly come up with a way of helping people overcome the limitations of dyslexia simply by playing video games. These games were 'learning in disguise', as one facilitator described it.

This was the chapter on the Fast ForWord Program and I became interested in it for application to my own practice.

Back then my hogwash radar was still in its infancy and like many in the field, I felt optimistic that some sort of 'breakthrough' existed. I went to hear Doidge speak and undertook the training (and licence-fee paying) so that I could begin using Fast ForWord in my practice.

I couldn't wait to show my students that they no longer needed so much of the careful one-on-one tuition they were used to, but instead that they could play video games! My enthusiasm even extended to the local schools, several of whom allowed me to set Fast ForWord up on my students' computers so that they could play and learn during literacy blocks. It was set to take the town by storm and have all those unfortunate kids happily reading, writing and spelling in no time!

This is what happened:

1. The children found the games boring.
2. No discernible improvement took place in the abilities of any of the kids.
3. I abandoned Fast ForWord within six months and went back to regular tutoring.

Independent research has repeatedly found no evidence that Fast ForWord is an effective intervention for language or reading difficulties (Strong, Torgerson, Torgerson & Hulme 2010).

I had allowed myself to be convinced by a very authoritative speaker.

On the flipside, I am often questioned on my own authority in this field. I'll admit, I'm a bit of a strange case, having only done a bachelor's degree in linguistics. I have kept myself as well-trained as possible and I have a wealth of experience, but I don't hold a PhD.

That's why it's important to be able to back your claims. Everything I say I try to make sure I can support. This takes the perception of 'authority' out of the equation and everybody wins.

Anecdotal evidence

Positive stories from friends, authority figures or family are powerfully persuasive (Figure 17.7). Back in the day when research and wide-ranging views weren't readily available online, we had to rely heavily on word of mouth to evaluate the truth of claims.

Human culture has always been rich in stories, tales and myths. We are hard-wired for anecdotes and as such, are particularly vulnerable to them. However, as Ben Goldacre states in the highly recommended Ted Talk *Battling Bad Science*, 'The plural of anecdote is not data' (2011).

If you put all the different types of evidence into a pyramid, with the least reliable at the bottom and the most reliable at the top, you'll find anecdotes occupy that bottom rung. Because it's easier to tell stories than it is to design reliable studies, anecdotes are the most abundant of all available information sources.

Next comes expert opinion. It's relatively hard to become an expert at something. It takes time and experience. But even those who have truly earned their expert status can still get it wrong. It is not until you put a theory to the test, as in the three upper rungs of the pyramid that you begin to remove human fallibility.

A single case study is a good indicator that a theory is at least workable in one instance. This can then be re-tested with other people in a trial. The best trials are randomised controlled trials, where participants are shielded from the possibility of the placebo effect (see Chapter 18).

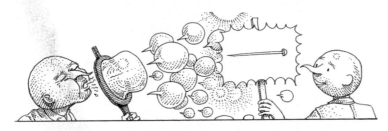

Figure 17.7 Anecdotal evidence

Some academics spend a great deal of time collecting these studies and looking at the combined results. This is called a meta-analysis and yields the most reliable data. But if you compare the time, money and effort needed to reach this peak to the time and effort it takes to tell an 'it worked for me' story, you'll also see why anecdotes are so plentiful and meta-analyses so scarce (Figure 17.8).

How some use anecdotes to fool others

Anecdotes are the stock in trade for snake oil merchants the world over. Being a vocal anti-woo type, I have often been engaged in some kind of war of ideas with some business person or other trying to hawk their dodgy goods.

When challenged on the efficacy of what they're selling or promoting, I often get asked if I have had the training or used the product myself. My answer is, 'Why would it matter? Why would a brief view by one person matter? My question to *you* is, why you think you don't need to see research before you throw your weight behind something? Are you not aware of the how science works?'

Anecdotes are very tempting and it makes sense to listen to the experiences and opinions of others. But please, I beg you, make your decisions based on more than just stories.

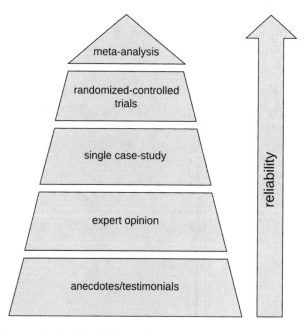

Figure 17.8 Reliability scale

Figure 17.9 Special pleading

Special pleading

This is where a person who knows better argues for an unjustified exception. It's also known as the application of a double standard (Figure 17.9).

How some try to fool others with special pleading

I have a lovely, warm, funny, kind friend. Actually, I have a few, but the one I'm talking about is constantly annoyed by my refusal to accept her special pleading.

I live in a semi-rural part of Australia called the Mornington Peninsula. We have an abundance of native wildlife and we owe part of that to a law which has been in place since 2008, stating that domestic cats must be confined to their owners' property at all times, either indoors or in approved cat-runs.

I keep my cats indoors, not just because that's the law, but because I like them to be safe from dogs, cars and disease. I like the birds that come to my garden. My cats are happy and we deal with the litter trays as a small price to pay for the win-win.

My friend, and many others, allow their cats to roam. Whenever I protest this, she tells me that her cats don't kill. She is aware that other cats kill. She is aware of their prey-drive and their sharp teeth and claws specially evolved for killing. But her cats are different.

This is special pleading. Even if, by some miracle, her cats weren't killers, she couldn't possibly know that for sure. So why not give the birds and the lizards in her garden the benefit of the doubt? Her cats would be safer and we wouldn't argue so much.

How special pleading is used in education

There are times when people use special pleading to protect their brand. This is used in education constantly, and especially when a brand's techniques fall outside what is generally accepted as the most effective way to instruct.

Beware an author quoting research that defends the company's position whilst at the same time imploring its adherents to ignore research that doesn't agree with their view. 'We don't know why it works, it just works' is not good enough in education.

References

Snow, C. E., & Juel. C. (2007). Teaching Children to Read: What Do We Know about How to Do It? In M. J. Snowling & C. Hulme (Eds.), *The Science of Reading: A Handbook*, pp. 224–35. Malden, MA: Blackwell.

Strong, G. K., Torgerson, C. J., Torgerson, D., & Hulme, C. (2010). A Systematic Meta-Analytic Review of Evidence for the Effectiveness of the 'Fast ForWord' Language Intervention Program. *Journal of Child Psychology and Psychiatry*, 52(3), 224–35. doi:10.1111/j.1469-7610.2010.02329.x

Vigen, T. (2015). *Spurious Correlations*. Manhattan: Hachette.

CHAPTER 18

Fooling ourselves
Cognitive bias

People take great pains to convince us of their untruths. Sometimes it's hard, but in many cases it's easy. This is because humans often come pre-loaded with flaws in their thinking called cognitive bias.

We tend to judge situations based on what we have already experienced and this can be exploited. Cognitive bias evolved to help us make snap decisions in situations where there isn't much time, but it is not always rational.

Even seasoned scientists have to be careful not to let their own biases cloud their research. This chapter will illustrate some common biases and how to avoid them so that the daunting task of selecting and evaluating methods of instruction or intervention is slightly easier. It is also intended as something of an answer to the mystery of poor ideas and their persistence.

Confirmation bias

I started thinking that X might be true. Then my friend told me a story where X happened. That means X must be true (Figure 18.1).

When you already believe something, it is easier to accept other people's stories confirming your beliefs than it is to examine the truthfulness of such stories. Anecdotal evidence is highly persuasive when confirmation bias is present.

Hypothetically speaking, imagine the all too common scenario of a parent seeking help for their child who is lagging behind in reading. I speak to a dozen parents in this situation on a regular basis. Some of them ask me if I run computerised 'brain training' sessions and programs.

Sometimes, parents have heard of brain training exercises and can see how it might be possible to improve their child's ability to read by going through a program offering this kind of thing. The seed of the idea is present.

Now imagine that the parent talks to a friend who says that they have personally experienced improvement from such exercises. Imagine the parent

Figure 18.1 Confirmation bias

asking around and hearing about other people who have also felt that improvements have been made.

What they come to me with, in that scenario, is a very thick layer of almost impenetrable bias. No amount of research, evidence, papers, statements, statistics or *anything* is likely to change their conviction that electronic brain training works. Too much of their original opinion has been confirmed by trusted sources.

My only option is to listen and outline why my old-fashioned, direct, explicit instruction in reading and writing could also be helpful.

That's why testimonials are so powerful. They take a wishful thought and dramatically increase its perceived validity, just through the telling of a story. Anecdotal evidence and confirmation bias form a strong adhesive bond and can stick ideas to people like superglue.

A good inoculation against confirmation bias is to seek and listen to opinions that clash with your own from time to time. It is very easy to sit in a bubble, surrounded by people who agree with you. Social media has increased this possibility a hundredfold, giving the means for a million different echo chambers to exist.

This is why it is important to understand multidisciplinary convergence – that is, when several fields, over time, come to the same conclusions about a theory. Reading instruction is one of the finest examples of such a convergence.

Now that you've read about confirmation bias, I'm sure you'll be seeing it everywhere.

The Dunning-Kruger effect

People who lack knowledge in a subject have no way of knowing the extent of their knowledge, or lack thereof (Figure 18.2). This can sometimes lead them to vastly overestimate their competence. Conversely, experts can tend to assume others share their expertise, so can sometimes not explain their thinking clearly enough to have lay people understand them.

Figure 18.2 The Dunning-Kruger effect

Experimental psychologists David Dunning and Justin Kruger observed this bias and wrote extensively about its effect. It stems either from an error in self-judgement or from an error in judgement of others (Dunning 2011).

In education, teachers often rate their abilities and knowledge much higher than actual tests of those abilities reveal. In a not atypical survey of teachers in New Zealand in 2018, over 600 primary school teachers responded to questions gauging their perceived phonic use and comparing it to their phonic knowledge (Chapman, Greaney, Arrow & Tunmer 2018).

90% of the respondents said they were indeed using phonics during literacy instruction, but when tested only 40% actually used phonics to help prompt reading. The other 60% used contextual cues or something even less specific, thinking this counted as phonics.

If teachers feel they are doing the best job possible yet are not familiar with what constitutes the best job possible, not only are they doing a disservice to struggling readers, but they are also not likely to seek change.

Researcher Keith Stanovich and others make the point very well in a 2004 paper on the subject:

> Reading experts agree by consensus that if teachers are poorly calibrated and significantly overestimate their knowledge of important reading related information, they will not seek to acquire or be open to new constructs presented in the context of professional development.
>
> (Cunningham, Perry, Stanovich & Stanovich 2004)

The more cult-like, drawn out and isolating a teacher training program is, the more likely its trainees will fall prey to not knowing what they don't know.

It isn't just a problem with low ability, though. The other side of the Dunning-Kruger effect is the case of the expert who is unable to gauge their expertise in comparison to lay people. This can cause them to assume that tasks or concepts that they find easy are also easy for others.

In education there is much talk of the 'research to practice gap'. Sometimes valid, important findings fail to make it into everyday practice because they are presented in ways that people can't readily understand. Take the idea of orthographic mapping. Though I knew about the process intuitively from experience and observation, I was unaware that there was a name for this or that anyone had written about it until I began researching this book. Yet Linnea Ehri has been writing about it since 2005. I don't blame Ehri, of course, but I do see a need for a middle-agent to help bring scientific understanding to the coalface (Figure 18.3).

I also see this in schools when it comes to spelling. Some folks are just plain lucky and only have to see a word once or twice to have that word perfectly stored in their memory forever. People with these talents are often drawn to the teaching profession. At the other end of the scale, there are people who have massive difficulty storing and retrieving spelling patterns. It's the luck of the draw, but the misfortune of not having an aptitude for spelling can be compounded when your teacher is one of the lucky ones.

Great spellers often do not know how they became great spellers. They just are. When they become teachers, they can sometimes find it hard to explain to anyone how to improve their spelling, since this is something they've never had to consciously do. Those who struggle with spelling can often appear deliberately frustrating or even *lazy* to superior spellers. Just because it seems easy and natural to you, doesn't mean that it's the same for others. This is why it's important for teachers to thoroughly understand the process of learning to read and write. Teacher training institutions fall painfully short on making sure this happens.

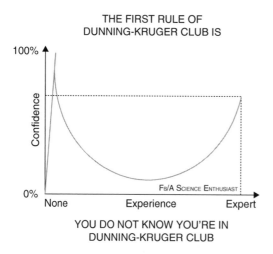

Figure 18.3 Dunning-Kruger Club graph. Courtesy of Dan Broadbent @SciEnthusiast

The anchoring bias

Sometimes, the first piece of information that we hear about something is the one that we rely on most for making subsequent decisions, even if that information is flawed (Figure 18.4).

When I graduated from university, the first training in literacy instruction I ever had said that you should teach children to read by introducing, in a careful sequence, the sounds and symbols of English, and that if you taught students to blend and segment these sounds and symbols, and if you gave them sufficient practice, they would be able to read and write words of greater and greater complexity. This is systematic synthetic phonics. I didn't know the name for it yet and I wasn't aware of the great debate around it, but it certainly made sense, given my background in linguistics, and it gave me a degree of success that I was pleased with.

Fortunately, that first piece of information, on which I based most of the work of my career, happened to be well supported by research.

I often wonder what I would have done with information which said that reading is a 'meaning-making' exercise and that children learned to read through 'sampling' just enough writing in order to bring their own knowledge to the story.

Would that have anchored my view too, or at some point, would have I said, 'Hang on a minute, this is nonsense'?

I'm hoping the latter, but in reality, vast numbers of people in education are walking around clinging to the first piece of information they heard about reading and that information is usually whole language-laden. Sadly, due to the tendency of teacher training institutes and publishers to play down the role of explicit, direct, early code-based instruction, false, outdated ideas are often the first thing teachers hear. They then become anchored by this and can experience just enough success to continue on in these beliefs for their entire career.

Figure 18.4 Anchoring bias

Figure 18.5 Halo effect

The halo effect

I like this person so what they're selling must be acceptable to me (Figure 18.5).

This, ladies and gentlemen, is the bias that every snake oil peddler, every evangelical TV host, every politician and PR spin merchant relies on to sell you things.

For an example outside of education, consider the case of a big, bronzed, perfect-toothed, shiny, handsome 'chef' in Australia. He is a reality TV star and an irresistible personality. His success is huge and he is a well-loved multi-millionaire.

The only problem is that he has said the following evidence-free things:

- Chicken liver and bone-broth is a suitable DIY baby milk formula.
- Sunscreen is dangerous, but surf-mud is a good sun protection.
- Calcium from dairy products can remove the calcium from your bones.
- Vegetable oils are unnatural and should be labeled 'sickness in a tub'.
- Fluoride in water is bad for you.

He continues to enjoy large book sales and a host spot on one of TV's highest rating reality shows. That's some halo effect from a person who makes dangerous statements like the above.

Similarly, the halo effect is rife in education. When a shiny, PR-trained front-person sucks you into their personal narrative and then relieves you of your well-earned bucks for programs and resources that make zero or a negative impact, you have suffered from the halo effect.

So if you feel yourself drawn to a person selling you a product or intervention, look out for their halo. It's okay to like someone, but whatever you buy from them or agree to has to stand on its own merits.

Check your bias before buying:

1. If the product or method aligns with what you already understand about the field, don't leave it at that. Can it be backed by evidence?

2. If it doesn't align with what you understand, seek to find out why; could there be an alternative hypothesis?
3. Be careful what you wish for! Do you really *really* wish it were true? Wishful thinking clouds judgement.

References

Chapman, J. W., Greaney, K. T., Arrow, A. W., & Tunmer, W. E. (2018). Teachers' Use of Phonics, Knowledge of Language Constructs, and Preferred Word Identification Prompts in Relation to Beginning Readers. *Australian Journal of Learning Difficulties*, 23(1), 87–104. doi:10.1080/19404158.2018.1467937

Cunningham, A. E., Perry, K. E., Stanovich, K. E., & Stanovich, P. J. (2004). Disciplinary Knowledge of K-3 Teachers and Their Knowledge Calibration in the Domain of Early Literacy. *Annals of Dyslexia*, 54(1), 139–67. doi:10.1007/s11881-004-0007-y

Dunning, D. G. (2011). The Dunning-Kruger Effect: On Being Ignorant of One's Own Ignorance. In J. M. Olson & M. P. Zanna (Eds.), *Advances in Experimental Psychology*, Vol. 44, pp. 247–96. San Diego: Academic Press.

Ehri, L. C. (2005). Development of Sight Word Reading: Phases and Findings. In M. J. Snowling & C. Hulme (Eds.), *The Science of Reading: A Handbook*, pp. 135–54. Oxford: Blackwell Publishing.

CHAPTER 19

Snake oil
The disappointing truth

Back in the 19th century, Chinese migration to the United States saw a massive upswing. Projects like the Transcontinental Railway required an influx of labour, seeing some 180,000 Chinese workers travel to the States. With them came many traditional medicines, and one in particular that had a lasting effect on our vocabulary, if not our medical system.

It was made from oil derived from the fat of Chinese water snakes. Rich in omega-3, this oil had the kind of anti-inflammatory properties a tired and stiff railroad worker could benefit from. As such, it soon caught the attention of the wider community.

Fast forward a couple of decades and the Rattlesnake King, Clark Stanley, was making a tidy profit selling bottles of Stanley's Snake Oil for an astonishing range of ailments. The mixture, he loudly proclaimed, was able to provide relief from 'all pain and lameness, rheumatism, neuralgia, sciatica, sprains, bunions, and sore throat, for bites of animals and reptiles, for all pains and aches in flesh, muscle and joints, as a relief for tic douloureux, and as a cure for partial paralysis of the arms and of the lower limbs ...' (United States Bureau of Chemistry 1914).

There were two problems with this miracle cure:

1. It didn't actually work.
2. When tested by the newly established Food and Drug Administration, it was found to contain no actual snake oil at all, but a mix of beef fat, red pepper, camphor and turpentine.

The phrase 'snake oil' to describe fraudulent treatments had been born. A mildly good idea with limited application had been seized upon by an entrepreneur and marketed to desperate people. Thank goodness that doesn't happen anymore.

Except it does. Snake oil makes it necessary for highly qualified, eminent, busy professionals to take time out of their normal jobs and write books about it as a warning to others. Ben Goldacre's *Bad Science* and Caroline Bowen and Pamela Snow's *Making Sense of Interventions for Children with Developmental Disorders* are two such recent publications. They come highly recommended.

21st-century education, like health, has a snake oil problem. Consumers want quick fixes for conditions they don't fully understand. There are plenty of snake oil peddlers waiting to cash in.

Bowen and Snow describe the relative ease with which desperate parents can be deceived:

> *[The] meticulous process of screening, detailed assessment, and choosing an intervention that matches the child's needs is lacking in many fad interventions, where all a parent need do is 'self-diagnose' a difficulty ... locate a product or service, pay the money and live with the consequences.*

Most schools receive government funding of some type, so selling an education or intervention product to parents and schools can be a licence to print money. Lack of teacher knowledge about what actually constitutes research and evidence results in millions wasted annually on terrific sounding programs and equipment that do virtually no good whatsoever.

Time, hope and money are three resources in short supply. Judicious use of reading intervention can result in life-changing, long-lasting improvements. But if programs or interventions are low in quality, the results can be life-changing and long-lasting in detrimental ways.

Sadly, there are predators in every walk of life who don't mind if they eat up time, dash hopes and walk away with unearned money.

There are several reasons people sell, promote or defend products with questionable benefit:

1. Sellers like making easy money from desperate people.
2. Sellers enjoy the power that their brand's followers bestow on them.
3. Buyers have made an investment (emotional and/or financial) in the product themselves and don't want to feel wrong.

This chapter is going to explore some popular products and ideas in education that don't have an evidence base. They persist because of 1, 2 or 3 above.

Humans are vastly complex, and the human mind is a powerful thing. There really is substance to the phrase 'mind over matter'. Our thoughts have an enormous influence on our worlds.

There are also a couple of fascinating phenomena that are useful to be aware of, concerning why things appear to work and yet have no evidence to support them.

The placebo effect: Every bite counts

Origin: Latin *placebo* 'I shall please'; first recorded in medicine in 1785 as 'a medicine given to please the patient rather than give cure'.

Thousands of experiments in dozens of fields have shown that people can experience real improvement in a vast array of conditions simply by *believing* their treatment will be helpful.

When medicines go through clinical trials, they are subjected to *placebo-controlled* trials wherever possible. This is when one experimental group receives the treatment and the other experimental group receives a fake treatment, such as a sugar pill.

We are also prone to the placebo effect when there is a lot of ceremony, theatre and cultural significance built into the treatment. Think witch doctors, traditional Chinese medicine and crystal healing.

Snake oil peddlers in education absolutely thrive on the placebo effect. But here's the problem: When children are struggling with reading and writing, the window of opportunity to provide meaningful, effective intervention is relatively small. Making them believe their intervention is helpful will only go a little way to improving. It will not be particularly sustainable.

I once heard a nutritionist put forward a great argument for giving small children the best quality, most nourishing food. She said something like, 'Children's stomachs are small: every bite counts'. This is equally true for literacy instruction or intervention. When you have a child's attention, make your input count. Using over-elaborate songs and actions, reminder pictures or kooky characters with complicated stories is sweet and nice, but it's junk! There is very little value in anything that detracts from teaching and practising straight, frank, discrete letter–sound correspondences.

'But what about engagement?' I hear you cry! 'My students would be so much more willing to do the work when I've got all the bells ringing and the whistles blowing!' My response? I could also get my children to 'engage' with all their dinners if I put ice cream and cake on their plates and sprinkled everything with sugar. But you know what? I don't, because I'm trying to help them grow their bodies in a healthy, sustainable way. And sometimes, it doesn't make me particularly popular, but I'm the adult, so I'll trade my temporary popularity for their long-term health if I have to.

Those things which distract from explicit code-based teaching and repetitive, targeted practice are junk. Being satisfied with placebos or shirking the hard work of teaching the code is the same as thinking you are nourishing your child by giving them a diet of junk food. Every bite counts.

The Hawthorne effect

This effect is named after a series of experiments in the Western Electric Company in Hawthorne, Massachusetts, in 1924. Experimenters set out to test how certain changes to the factory might increase productivity.

The workers were divided into two groups, and at first, experimenters were pleasantly surprised to find that the group whose lighting was made brighter out-produced the control group whose lighting remained the same. Further controlled studies revealed that other changes in workers' conditions had a similar effect.

Even when conditions were changed back again to the *original* settings, productivity in the changed group outstripped that of the control group (Gillespie 1992).

The point was, that the *changes* themselves, not the content of the changes, were perceived by the workers to be beneficial. So the workers, feeling listened to, were willing to go the extra distance for what they saw as a caring management.

If you take a child who, for reasons they cannot understand, lags behind their peers in reading, and make them feel understood, cared about and listened to, they will most likely make an effort to improve. This is the one positive element common to all small group and individual intervention programs.

A new, but important-feeling program of instruction does have a temporary influence on the productivity of teachers and learners. It can even give a brief advantage over their everyday system of instruction. However, sustainable gains come from being taught what is necessary for independence. Being made to *feel* a certain way has its limits.

Coloured lenses/vision therapy

> *Ineffective, controversial methods of treatment such as vision therapy may give parents and teachers a false sense of security that a child's learning difficulties are being addressed, may waste family and/or school resources, and may delay proper instruction or remediation.*
>
> Learning Disabilities, Dyslexia, and Vision (2009)

Probably the most widespread placebo effect in literacy intervention is the coloured glasses/overlays scam. One of the first recommendations I make to families worried about a child's reading progress is to get their sight and hearing tested by a regular optometrist and their GP. We need to know if the child can see and hear within normal limits.

Aside from astigmatism and short- and long-sightedness, there are two major additional conditions that can affect literacy acquisition: convergence insufficiency and amblyopia. They are real and can improve with proper treatment.

Convergence insufficiency is the inability to keep the two eyes working together while working at a near distance. It can result in double vision, headaches, words moving around on the page and blurriness when reading. Home- and computer-based exercises under the care of a suitably qualified professional can correct this.

Amblyopia, colloquially known as *lazy eye*, occurs when one eye experiences a normal view, but the other eye experiences a blurred view, leading the brain to only process the normal view. This can lead to vision loss unless corrected. Patches and eye drops to strengthen the weak eye are usually prescribed.

Then there is disease-mongering. Once upon a time, a psychologist called Helen Irlen believed she had made a breakthrough in helping struggling readers. Placing sheets of transparent, but tinted acetate over the top of texts resulted in some of her students declaring that reading had become easier for them. There can be a slight placebo effect when a person tries on coloured lenses or uses overlays. They sometimes report improved ability to see the letters on a page (cutting glare from overhead lights has a lot to do with this) and hopeful parents delight in the fact that their children have a renewed interest in books. The effect is mostly short-lived since it does nothing to remediate problems in the language system, which is at the basis of most reading difficulties.

Claims about coloured lenses and reading are easily testable, and it didn't take long or indeed much effort, to conclude that coloured lenses were no better than a placebo. This didn't stop what happened next.

Powerful testimonials about 'Irlen lenses', scientific-sounding in-house but unpublished research studies and the charisma of the company's leader resulted in 170 Irlen Clinics throughout the world, and according to their website, over 10,000 'educators' trained in the Irlen Method.

That's a lot of children and families investing in placebos.

Irlen's Syndrome, Scotopic Sensitivity Syndrome, visual stress and anything else where a 'practitioner' recommends coloured lenses or overlays or expensive eye exercise regimes to improve reading is a scam and generally acknowledged by peak bodies of ocular professionals as not worthy.

Listening therapy/auditory programs

Seeking help for a struggling reader can lead parents and teachers down all kinds of weird and wonderful paths. What would your reaction be if you came to me, looking for a solution to a child's reading problems, and I started testing their earlobes? What if I showed you a report saying that your child's earlobes were sub-standard and that if you gave me a large sum of money, I would work on those earlobes, give you some earlobe exercises to do at home and would run further tests on the earlobes at a later date to make sure the treatment was working?

After all, the earlobes are involved in directing sound towards your auditory cortex, so if you work on optimising them, surely that would make a difference to your child's literacy.

Perhaps you could buy some earlobe overlays in different fabrics and textures, depending on your child's carefully calibrated sensitivities and preferences.

Or would you prefer me to test, work on and re-test their reading and spelling?

Having trouble distinguishing sounds from one another in words and struggling to relate them to printed symbols is a problem that originates in the complex network of language systems in the brain. Programs that say they improve reading and spelling by working on some vague auditory or visual system might as well be earlobe programs.

There are several on the market. My advice is to avoid them. There are no shortcuts to learning the alphabetic code with automaticity.

'Brain training'

Or, as well-informed professionals like to call it: *learning* (Castles and McArthur, 2012). Programs and products that promise neurological improvement as their *main* product are not quite what they seem.

If you think about it, *all* learning takes place in the brain. The crude comparison of a brain to a muscle that needs exercising fails to address the fact that the brain is *always* working.

We do not yet have sufficient information to provide exercises that activate precise brain structures. That's wishful, futuristic thinking that is in no way reflective of reality.

Physical movement programs

If you want a child's reading and writing to improve, what they have to do is read and write. I'm not sure why I need to keep saying this.

And yet the oddest approaches to literacy still abound and their authors make millions. Saying that certain exercises or physical activity will raise literacy is simply not true. There is no research to support this and because it's quite nice and doesn't particularly *harm* children, adults will make time and pay money for it.

Crossing the mid-line, working on primitive reflexes, metronome training and chiropractic neurology: none of these has been shown, under any conditions, to positively affect reading and writing.

How to protect against snake oil

Nothing is more important than targeted, evidence-based intervention when a child struggles with literacy. Time, money, effort and self-esteem are in short supply and cannot be wasted on placebos. This is doubly significant when we already have plenty of information on how best to help someone read and write.

So if you ever feel ashamed or embarrassed that you believed something that wasn't true, please don't forget: you can be smart, educated, well brought up, compassionate and truth-seeking and you can still be taken in by utter claptrap if you happen to have an utter claptrap-shaped hole in your life at the time the utter claptrap is being offered. And it takes all forms.

If you take offence because I've mentioned something you actually like, please remember, it's nothing personal. The following checklist is here for your protection, not your humiliation.

1. **All learning is brain training.** If you hear the words 'brain training' in any marketing of any product in education, my advice to you is grab your wallet and run in the opposite direction.
2. **There is no panacea.** If a company lists a wide range of disorders as treatable by one method, chances are it's not true.
3. **Anecdotes do not equal data.** Consider the fact that one or two very sincere, very enthusiastic stories about a product does not make that product necessarily good.
4. **Transfer and generalisation rarely happens.** If a product claims to improve reading and writing but does not actually include the act of reading and writing, there's not a lot of hope that it will work.
5. **Your financial investment affects you.** If you have to pay a large sum of money for a product or treatment, please be aware that your financial investment might cloud your judgement of the efficacy of that product. We don't like to feel that we've been silly with our money.
6. **Placebos have limits.** Remember, placebos wear off and the underlying causes remain.

7. **Every bite counts.** Seeking alternative or complementary treatments may look like they're doing no harm, but it's quite common for a child to blame themselves when things don't seem to be working. When things are working and the cause of that is misattributed, this too has risks.

8. **'Coming soon' often means 'never coming'.** The older and larger a company is, the more obligation they have to back up their claims with independent research. If you are told that there's research 'in the pipeline', ask precisely when the research is expected and follow up on this before making any large time or financial commitments.

References

Bowen, C., & Snow, P. (2017). *Making Sense of Interventions for Children with Developmental Disorders*. Guildford: J&R Press.

Castles, A., & McArthur, G. (2012). 'Brain Training' … or Learning as We Like to Call It. *The Conversation*, 5 October. http://theconversation.com/brain-training-or-learning-as-we-like-to-call-it-9951.

Gillespie, R. (1992). Manufacturing Knowledge: A History of the Hawthorne Experiments. *American Journal of Sociology*, 98(1), 201–03. doi:10.1086/229990

Goldacre, B. (2009). *Bad Science*. London: Fourth Estate.

Learning Disabilities, Dyslexia, and Vision. (2009). *Pediatrics*, 124(2), 837–44. doi:10.1542/peds.2009-1445

United States Bureau of Chemistry. (1914). *Service and Regulatory Announcements* (Vol. 1). US Government Printing Office.

CHAPTER 20

Diagnosis
Dyslexia

There's nothing socially acceptable about a pervasive, lifelong neurological condition that affects the sufferer's ability to deal with print. Pundits in the field still try to perpetuate the myth that dyslexia is socially acceptable. Take children's author Mem Fox, whose opinion is not uncommon in teacher training institutions the world over:

There exist highly privileged children in our society who cannot read, or will not read. It's not difficult to find out why: they have television; they have toys, computer games, personal devices, bikes and all the trappings of a well-off childhood; but they don't have books. These children often have a reading problem at school that their panic-stricken parents disguise under the socially acceptable label of dyslexia.

The word *dyslexia* comes from the Greek rood *dys*, which means 'bad, difficult, abnormal' (e.g. *dysfunctional, dystopia, dystrophy*), and *lex*, which means 'word' (*lexicon, lexicography*). Dyslexia means 'word problems'.

Apart from the crippling effects that dyslexia has in the classroom, diminished social and emotional wellbeing are often suffered by people with this condition. Their suffering is multiplied if, on top of it, they are not well taught.

Decades of discussion and refinement have led to much agreement on the definition, diagnosis and treatment of dyslexia. That's not to say that the science on the condition is settled. In fact, there are still many unanswered questions and, sadly, a lot of room for misinterpretation and misleading answers.

Problems arise when the term *dyslexia* is used to refer to every struggling or low-progress reader. The meaning of dyslexia becomes diluted if all of these children are given that label.

Reading difficulties are a possible sign of dyslexia, but it is a bad idea to form a diagnosis on that basis alone. Screening for other signs and symptoms of dyslexia before testing is therefore recommended.

This is the main reason that many esteemed researchers and practitioners prefer not to use the term *dyslexia*, but instead would have us say *reading difficulties, reading disability* or *reading impairment* (Bowen & Snow 2017).

128

I also understand that the name is less important than the search for the most effective solutions, but I don't think the term *dyslexia* has quite outlived its usefulness yet.

With the greatest respect to some of my colleagues in the field, I still must assert that having the term *dyslexia* is necessary for a number of reasons:

1. Dyslexia affects more than just reading. It also compromises the ability to spell, write and pronounce words.
2. Having one word is searchable, identifiable and helps to succinctly communicate the cluster of symptoms associated with the condition.
3. Those who fall within the spectrum of symptoms have a name for their difficulties. This is often a relief, especially when reading and spelling are commonly used to judge intelligence. Knowing their poor spelling is due to dyslexia helps people overcome the social limitations of the condition.

Many countries now have dyslexia associations to help advise and guide parents and teachers on this difficult journey. These associations are often made up of parents and practitioners whose aim is to help others advocate for themselves and their children.

Dyslexia myths and facts

There are plenty of facts about dyslexia and just as many myths. If in doubt, consulting the International Dyslexia Association is a good starting point. They will be able to advise you who to contact in your country for local support.

In the meantime, knowing a little more about what dyslexia is and what it is not is an important first step. (See Figure 20.2 at the end of the chapter for a summary of the following information.)

Dyslexia is neurological

This means that the condition originates in the brain. More importantly, in the language centres of the brain – not the eyes, not the ears, not the reflexes nor the digestive system.

Scientists have good reason to believe that dyslexia can be passed on genetically. Difficulties with print often run in families.

This runs counter to some claims that dyslexia can be caused. Evidence for dyslexia actually being the result of something other than the way the brain is structured, is poor to non-existent. Some of the supposed causes of dyslexia have been claimed as:

- excessive screen time
- poor diet
- low IQ
- phonics (!)
- not being read to as an infant
- a problem with the eyes
- a problem with the ears

People who have dyslexia may well fall into some or all of the categories above. They may also have a centre-parting or freckles. None of it causes dyslexia.

Dyslexia is developmental

A developmental disorder is a chronic disability, usually starting in childhood, that affects one or more major life functions. In the case of dyslexia, the ability to learn and use written language is impaired.

Because it is developmental, it is not just going to 'go away'. Children do not outgrow dyslexia. The aspects of written language that dyslexia affects vary between individuals in their range and severity. These can be addressed, with skilled intervention, but the disorder itself never goes away.

This is why dyslexia 'cures' have no validity. A developmental disorder is not a disease to be 'cured'.

Dyslexia is pervasive

This means that precisely because it is neurological, developmental and heritable, dyslexia can affect anyone from any background.

No one section of the population, however you slice it up, is more prone to dyslexia. That is not to say that some people don't receive better support.

Dyslexics from more privileged homes are more likely to receive early diagnosis and intervention, although this wasn't always the case. Dyslexia awareness is still in its infancy, relatively speaking. You only need look at Richard Branson's generation to see how even wealthy dyslexics used to be viewed. At boarding school, Branson said his dyslexia was '... treated as a handicap: my teachers thought I was lazy and dumb, and I couldn't keep up or fit in' (Branson 2017).

Dyslexia is treatable

Despite its permanence, dyslexia can be treated. The key to this is twofold:

1. Early reading instruction must contain well-delivered, systematic synthetic phonics.
2. Early screening, diagnosis and expert intervention must be available for those who need support to keep making progress.

Modern educators propose a model called *Response to Intervention* (RTI) to ensure that no child is left behind (Figure 20.1). This form of instruction is provided in tiers and caters not only to those in need of an academic boost but can be used to structure support for children with behavioural issues.

It involves the systematic implementation of research-based intervention at all levels and evaluates the child's response to that.

Dyslexia exists

Whatever the preferred term, neurologically-based, low progress reading and writing is a reality for many people. Still today, a lack of basic acknowledgement of the condition is the norm in Western schools.

Though it's not always possible to compare education and medicine, there is a good analogy here. In medicine, treatment that has a robust evidence base is more likely to be recommended. Medical practitioners have the freedom to be autonomous in their recommendations, but their rigorous training ensures that they prescribe the most effective paths known to them. As a result, conditions that we know much about, such as hypertension, peptic ulcers, HIV and skin cancer can now be addressed very successfully.

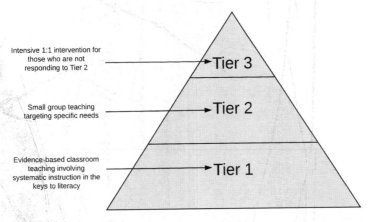

Figure 20.1 RTI pyramid

Educators are not obliged to adopt such rigour. There is a vast body of convergent research that shows very clearly what dyslexia is and what can be done about it. It's not a mystery and neither are its remedies. Yet schools and teachers are free to deny its existence, ignore it, take ineffective measures to reduce its impact or even avoid it altogether.

Now let's imagine if doctors were trained and allowed to act like some schools. It would be perfectly acceptable to do the following things:

1. Argue that the condition doesn't exist:

PATIENT: Doctor, I think I have high blood pressure.

DOCTOR: You have no such thing, you're simply lazy. Hypertension is just a trendy label to mask your poor work-ethic.

My practice is filled with exhausted, hard-working 'lazy' dyslexic children whose school reports implore then to 'concentrate' or 'make more effort'.

2. Ignore the condition:

HOSPITAL ADMINISTRATOR: I've never seen a case of peptic ulcers in this hospital. Nope, the ones with stomach pain and reflux are just unlucky. We tend to leave them alone.

The International Dyslexia Association estimates that 15–20% of the population have some dyslexic symptoms, making it difficult for them to achieve success in reading and/or writing in a typical classroom. The chance of an entire school having no dyslexic students is next to nil. Yet principals and teachers habitually claim that they know of none under their care who fit the description.

The fact is that there are reliable tests for dyslexia for children as young as five. There really is no excuse for any dyslexic child to get through school undiagnosed and unassisted.

3. Treat the condition with faddish, ineffective 'cures' and remedies:

DOCTOR: Because you're HIV positive I'd like you to try some crystals that can help with that. I also just read about a chap who ate carrots and nothing else for six months. Cured him completely. You might want to give that a go too.

PATIENT: I've tried the crystals and carrots and they're not helping.

DOCTOR: Look, I paid a lot of money for those crystals and my carrot training took a whole year! They're not working because you're obviously not trying hard enough to get better. I think you might be one of those incurables. Accept your fate!

4. Acknowledge the condition, but refuse to treat it, advising avoidance instead.

DOCTOR: Yes, my patient does have melanoma. I'm not going to treat it because I don't know how, but I *am* recommending he take up a profession where he's not exposed to the sun.

Secondary schools are particularly adept at pushing dyslexic children towards 'trades' or other career paths where reading and writing are required only minimally.

This reprehensible form of social engineering denies children the opportunity to pursue their true interests; strange behaviour in an educational climate which also ostensibly favours 'finding your element' and 'following your passion'.

Primary schools do bear the major responsibility for ensuring that children enter high school adequately prepared for its demands, it is true; but this doesn't mean that high schools should abandon those who struggle by tossing them towards a less challenging career.

High quality teacher training should arm teachers with the very latest information on what works and why.

Dyslexia is not a gift

I am not opposed to finding the positive in unpleasant situations, but I do not support the notion that dyslexia is somehow a gift.

As my dyslexic daughter puts it: 'My strengths are my own and not the result of dyslexia'.

I am very wary of labelling this difficulty as a gift. I don't think there is a single person alive who would deliberately choose to have dyslexia. Even in the most enlightened circles, humiliation, frustration, misunderstanding and struggle are frequent occurrences for dyslexics.

To say that dyslexics are 'out of the box thinkers', 'more creative', 'good at design', etc. is to place dangerous expectations on people already suffering. There is also no evidence whatsoever that this is true.

To say that as adults, those who struggled with dyslexia as children develop strength and resilience is a slap in the face for the thousands of people socially and economically disadvantaged by the condition, who didn't develop this strength, who perhaps even ended their lives because of it.

A child losing a parent early may also lead to some form of character strength, but nobody in their right mind would call that a gift.

What we say to one another as adults about this dubious 'gift' is important for how we frame dyslexia when talking to children. I know how strong the temptation is to have them 'own' the condition by pushing a false picture of some advantages of dyslexia, but false comfort is short-lived and hollow.

Here is what I say:

'You might need to work quite hard to learn to read and write fast, but it is not impossible, and we're going to give you all the help you need. Luckily you have lots of (insert individual positive traits, such as determination, humour, intelligence, creativity, patience, etc.) to help you out with that'.

Dyslexic children do not require 'special' or 'different' literacy instruction

Dyslexic or not, the path to reading follows the same trajectory from human to human. The stages on that path are complex and vary in length, but their order is the same.

In forums for teachers of whole language or 'balanced literacy' methods, I see, over and over again, the following kind of post:

Q: Help! A handful of my students have not made any progress this year and are still very far behind their classmates.

A: They are probably dyslexic.

Unfortunately, if your lessons have failed to help a student progress, it's your fault, not the child's. Dyslexic children can and should be taught to read. They and other slow progress readers do not deserve to become 'instructional casualties'. In fact, they should have been taught to read as part of the school's Tier 1 or Tier 2 approach in the first place. Too many children reach Tier 3 as a result of inadequate beginning reading instruction.

This also goes for so-called dyslexic fonts. Dyslexics do not require a special font to read with either. Widened spacing between letters can be helpful, but fonts designed specifically for dyslexic readers have no proven efficacy (Marinus et al. 2016).

The warning signs

As a parent or teacher, there are several ways you can evaluate low-progress readers/writers and make a decision about further testing. The key to this is *the earlier the better*. Low-progress readers/writers do not often 'grow out of it'.

You might want to consider referral to a qualified practitioner if the child in question exhibits the traits listed below, summarised from the Diagnostic and Statistical Manual of Mental Disorders, fifth edition (DSM-5).

- A persistent difficulty learning academic skills for at least six months despite intervention. In regard to dyslexia the areas of persistent weakness may include:
  1. inaccurate and slow reading
  2. difficulty with word decoding
  3. difficulty with the comprehension of text
  4. difficulty with spelling
  5. difficulties with grammar, punctuation and other writing skills

- The areas of weakness or skill impairment are significantly below expectation and impede academic progress.
- Learning difficulties may not be apparent until the demands of school are in excess of the student's progress (this can often happen when the demands of word-level reading increase, e.g. when books contain fewer pictures and more complex language).
- The academic and learning difficulties do not occur because of other issues such as intellectual, hearing, vision or mental health or due to inadequate instruction.

Inadequate instruction results in low progress reading with or without dyslexia. This is why the Response to Intervention model has to contain high quality reading instruction at all levels.

Who can help?

If you suspect dyslexia, having an assessment is a good idea, but taking action to boost the child's skills is also necessary.

Assessments can be costly and time-consuming. Make sure you ask around in approved local dyslexia groups regarding finding a practitioner who can assess and refer for intervention. Be wary of institutes that provide assessment *and* intervention. Some will diagnose disorders and treatment not backed by evidence, e.g. listening therapies or coloured lenses.

If a child is struggling with reading and writing, then a program of reading and writing needs to be implemented. Diet, exercise, sleep, kinesiology, 'brain training', chiropractic interventions, etc., do not directly address reading and writing.

The school

Ask your child's teacher to outline the type of assistance that is being provided in the classroom and the strategies that are being used to target any areas of concern.

The strategies need to take the form of explicit instruction in the components of literacy and need to be monitored to show progress.

If anyone is listening to the child read at school, ensure that they are not using a system of cueing by pictures or other comprehension strategies. Every time a child is robbed of the opportunity to decode a word all the way through, their progress suffers.

Speech-language professionals

Often, speech-language therapists are the first people to detect problems with language development in children. They are classified as health professionals, and as such, have scientific literacy built into their training. This makes them particularly immune to snake oil and particularly keen on evidence-based practice. They can assess, intervene and refer.

Educational psychologists

An educational psychologist is permitted to use certain tests and can make a formal diagnosis of dyslexia. Common practice in the field is to wait until the child has had 6 to 12 months of intervention targeting the specific areas of weakness, then assessing the child's response, prior to a formal diagnosis being made. This helps to differentiate the low progress readers from those with a developmental disorder.

Specialist tutors

Make sure your tutor has relevant qualifications, such as a teaching degree, a degree in linguistics, speech pathology or educational psychology. Ensure that they understand the components of reading and ask them what additional evidence-based programs they are trained in. One program only is rarely enough. Tutors who specialise in working with dyslexics need a large repertoire of techniques and perspectives to draw on.

If the tuition offered consists of 'brain training' or anything not directly involving reading and writing, consult your local dyslexia association before committing to it (Figure 20.2).

What dyslexia **is**	What dyslexia **is NOT**
neurological, i.e. it exists in brain structures	caused by external factors such as teaching phonics (this claim has been made!)
developmental, i.e. a condition that originates in childhood that has significant negative impact on certain functions	something that will just go away or that the person will 'grow out of'
pervasive, i.e. it affects people of every socio-economic background	a result of impoverished home circumstances (think Richard Branson)
treatable with evidence based, structured language instruction	curable through diet, brain-based learning programs etc.
real and present in a significant number of people	imaginary and an excuse for bad parenting
difficulty with words	reversal of letters, letters swimming around on a page, hearing problems, vision problems
unpleasant for the person with the condition	a gift
responsive to skilled teaching in the five pillars of literacy, just like every other person	needing some kind of 'special' education

Figure 20.2 Dyslexia fact and myth chart

References

American Psychiatric Association. (2013). *Diagnostic and Statistical Manual of Mental Disorders*, 5th ed. Washington, DC: Author.

Bowen, C., & Snow, P. (2017). *Making Sense of Interventions for Children with Developmental Disorders*. Guildford: J&R Press.

Branson, R. (2017). Richard Branson: Dyslexia is Merely Another Way of Thinking. *The Sunday Times*, 30 April. https://www.thetimes.co.uk/article/richard-branson-dyslexia-is-merely-another-way-of-thinking-8tlmgsndw

Fox, M. (2013). Flashing Screens or Turning Pages? *MemFox.com*, 26 September. https://memfox.com/for-parents/for-parents-flashing-screens-or-turning-pages/

Marinus, E., Mostard, M., Segers, E., Schubert, T. M., Madelaine, A., & Wheldall, K. (2016). A Special Font for People with Dyslexia: Does it Work and, If So, Why? *Dyslexia*, 22(3), 233–44. doi:10.1002/dys.1527

Teaching reading and writing

Overview

The ideas that follow are just that: ideas, rather than a set program. There are plenty of structured literacy programs on the market already. The tips and techniques here are for the children who need small group and individual intervention.

The setup

I have a specific setup in my practice consisting of a large whiteboard and magnetic tiles.

I use a mixture of the Lindamood LiPS magnetic tiles, the Read-Write Inc. tiles and my own self-produced suffixes and coloured tiles.

The diagram below shows the setup, which covers one of the walls of the office (Figure 21.1).

I use this setup to teach phonological awareness, phonics, and vocabulary.

The resources I use for fluency and comprehension are the Nanci Bell (2003) *Visualizing and Verbalizing Stories* Collection and the Dolores Hiskes (2007) *Reading Pathways* book.

The Survival List

My goal is to teach all of my students to read and write fluently. One of my tools is a list of words they need to learn as a priority. It's called the Survival List and it constitutes some tricky but common words and words containing patterns they find difficult to recall and use (Figure 21.2).

It is called the Survival List for two reasons:

1. Because knowing how to read and spell the words on their list will help students become fluent readers and writers as quickly as possible; and
2. Because the techniques used to learn these words can extend to other words with complex patterns. Students can learn these independently, once they know what to look out for.

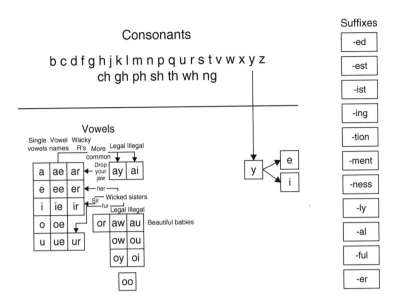

Figure 21.1 The practice setup

Every student's Survival List is different, but I take the words from a particular range of sources. I don't really subscribe to common word lists, because even though there are plenty of lists readily available, such as Dolch, Oxford or Fry, they contain a confusing mixture of simple and complex patterns. For instance, in the Dolch list, the word *big* (a simple 1:1 CVC pattern) is right there with *away* (a two-syllable word containing a digraph) and *said* (an unusual pronunciation of the digraph <ai>, which only really occurs in this word and in some accents in the word *again*, but which follows the grammatical/etymological pattern of *lay* and *pay*).

The number of times I see children being given homework requiring them to learn a mishmash of random patterns astonishes me. This is whole word learning and not viable for many.

As a starting point, I choose words that don't have a simple code structure and either place them in families containing similar patterns or use mnemonics. I teach a plain marking system to highlight the structure of the words.

The marking system goes like this:

- Underline letters that go together but represent one sound, e.g. <th>, <aw>, <igh>: pa<u>th</u>, s<u>aw</u>, n<u>igh</u>t.
- Put a cross underneath silent letters, e.g. house, crumb, autumn
- Indicate with a superscript arrow any letters having an effect on letters around it, e.g. wash, gate

	Word	Pattern	Family	Marking/mnemonic
1.	was	The W-Effect: when <w> precedes <a>, the <a> often makes an /ɒ/ sound (see illustration)	wash, wand, want, wander, wasp	An arrow pointing from the <w> to the double underlined <a>. w**a̲s̲**
2.	to	Belongs to a small family where the letter <o> makes an /ʊː/ sound	do, who, lose, shoe, move, prove, canoe	Double underline. t**o̲**
3.	there	<ere> making an 'air' sound, but also put into the same family as 'here'. These words contain the same pattern and are connected in meaning.	here, where	Underline the letters <h-e-r-e> in all three words. **here** w**here** t**here**
4.	said	<ay> to <aid> in the past tense	lay, pay	Double underline unusual sound of <a-i>. lay ⟶ laid pay ⟶ paid say ⟶ s**ai̲d**
5.	once	Builds up from the spelling of *one*, with the insertion of <c>, like the <c> in *twice*.	one, twice	A cross under Final Silent <e> with an arrow to show it making <c> say its second sound, /s/. Say letter names for spelling. onc**e** ✗
6.	they	<ey> making an /eɪ/ sound	grey (non-US), obey, prey, convey, survey	Double underline to show <ey> making an uncommon sound. th**ey̲**
7.	have	Final Silent E stopping the word from ending with an Illegal Letter	give, live, serve, five etc.	A cross under Final Silent <e> with an arrow to show that it is stopping the <v> from being at the end of the word. hav**e** ✗

Figure 21.2 The Survival List

	Word	Pattern	Family	Marking/mnemonic
8.	love	The letter <o> making an /ʌ/ sound	above, some, come, money, monkey, honey, other, mother	Double underline to show <o> is making an uncommon sound, cross under Final Silent <e> with an arrow to show that it is stopping the <v> from being at the end of the word. l<u>o</u>ve
9.	our	This is one of the supremely sticky spelling words. I have had to develop a technique of building up a memory of this word based on the word *you*, which is quickly learned.	<u>you</u> becomes <u>your</u> becomes <u>our</u>	When saying for spelling, I get students to say the letter names. Trying to link it with sounds, especially in Australian and English accents is next to useless. <o-u-r>
10.	eye	Another supremely sticky word that doesn't bear sounding out.	A rare instance of a lone existence. Just draw this picture and get students to practise saying the letter names.	eye
11.	friend	That strange <i> in the middle.		A cross under the silent <i>. "If you come round to my house I'll *fry* the end of the roast for you because you're my *friend*!". For spelling: fri...end. friend
12.	people	Silent <o> in the middle.	leopard	A cross under the silent <o> "When people see a leopard, they say 'o!'". people

Figure 21.2 Continued

	Word	Pattern	Family	Marking/mnemonic
13.	walk	Silent <l> and unusual sound of <a>	talk, chalk, stalk	Double underline for <a> and a cross underneath the silent <l>. w**a**lk
14.	any	<a> making an /e/ sound	many	Double underline the unusual /e/ sound: "Annie Needs You!" **a**ny
15.	buy	Silent <u>	build	Cross under the silent <u>. "Would u rather build or buy your dream home?" b**u**y
16.	write	Silent <w>	wrong, wrist, wrap, wreck	Cross under the silent w, arrow to show Final Silent E making the <i> say its name. write
17.	could	Unusual vowel sound, silent <l>	would, should	"Oh u lucky ducky". Nessy does a YouTube video on this that will drive you insane but your students won't forget it.
18.	does	Unusual vowel sound, -es third person singular suffix.	goes	go ⟶ goes do ⟶ does
19.	library	Collapsing syllable		"There's a *bra* in the library!" li-**bra**-ry
20.	too	Has two homophones (*two* and *to*)	Rather than teach this alongside the other two, I separate them out and teach this one to mastery first.	There are *too* many <o>s in this word!

Figure 21.2 Continued

The Survival List expands as our lessons progress. Students practise the words on the list two ways: first for spelling, then for reading. For spelling, they sound out the letters all the way to the end, pronouncing digraphs and trigraphs and silent letters as they go. For reading, they say the whole word. Take *night* for example:

FOR SPELLING: /n/-/aɪ/-/t/
FOR READING: *night*

References

Bell, N. (2003). *Visualizing and Verbalizing Stories.* San Luis Obispo, CA: Gander Publishing.
Hiskes, D. (2007). *Reading Pathways.* San Francisco, CA: Jossey-Bass.

CHAPTER 22

Teaching handwriting

Handwriting lessons, as a set of activities independent of reading and spelling, are an opportunity to establish habits for life. It is our responsibility to try to establish the best habits possible. This is why the activities below have longer-lasting, positive effects when practised daily for at least the first term of school and practised weekly for the whole first year.

Parents can be recruited to follow through with activities 1–3 at home. Both left- and right-handed students will benefit enormously from such guidance.

Left-handedness

Left-handed people comprise around 10% of the population. Despite popular opinion, there is little evidence that left-handed people differ in creative, spatial or artistic skills from right-handed people. They do, however, have more trouble with correct posture and pencil-grip if not taught consistently from a very young age. Special care should be taken to show left-handers how to sit and position their pencils.

Screenwriting

Screenwriting is a visual-kinaesthetic framework based on using an imaginary screen where words are written and manipulated.

The activities below are designed to help establish a visual framework. After that, the concept of the 'screen' and the visualisation of words can be used in spelling.

Activity 1: Setting up the screen

Ask students to draw in the air in front of them, a rectangular screen, like a TV or computer screen. It mustn't be too big or too small, because on that screen, they are going to do lots of writing of letters and words.

All drawing, including the drawing of the screen, is done with the index finger of the hand they use to write with.

To enhance visualisation, I often ask students to decorate the frame of the screen.

Activity 2: Practising big and small

Have students practise drawing big and small shapes and lines on their screens, whilst gaining mastery of the following terms:

- circle beginning at 2 on the clock
- tall line
- short line
- horizontal line
- diagonal line
- dot
- the direction that we read and write (left to right)

Activity 3: Start with what you know

If your students already know some words, have them write them on their screens for you. This could be a range of words, from their names to simple words they've seen and memorised.

Handwriting

When doing handwriting lessons, first have students practise the letter components on their screens, talking through their actions as they do them.

Activity 1: Positioning

I'm often surprised, when I'm visiting schools, to see children doing handwriting lessons in odd positions. Sometimes they are seated at an angle to the whiteboard. Sometimes they are sitting cross-legged on the floor. Sometimes their sitting position is never established or checked.

The way children sit when they are writing is extremely important, even during lessons when handwriting is not the focus. If they are seated improperly, they tend to get uncomfortable and can exhibit fidgeting or bodily aches and pains from incorrect posture.

Think about your preference, as an adult, when you have to hand-write something or take notes. Do you lie on cushions? Do you sit on the floor or facing away from the source of the information? I've yet to go into a professional development seminar laid out like an open-plan, progressive classroom. Instead, lecture theatres, seminar rooms and spaces where groups of people read, write and listen to an instructor are laid out in rows, facing the front. Why would that not be the case for classrooms?

During handwriting lessons especially, it is vital to establish the correct sitting position by requiring the following:

1. Students face the front of the classroom where they can clearly see the teacher.
2. Students sit with high heads, straight backs and both feet on the floor or footstool if they cannot reach the floor.
3. Both forearms rest on the table.
4. The wrist of the writing hand is straight and sits below the line they are writing on at all times. This is true for both left and right-handed children; if established early enough in left-handed children, difficulties with our left-to-right direction of writing do not surface.
5. The non-writing hand anchors the paper and moves it as needed.
6. The edge of the paper and the writing arm should be parallel, like train tracks.

A school I consult to invented this song to help with positioning:

'One, two, three, four,
Are your feet on the floor?
Five, six, seven, eight,
Is your back nice and straight?'

Practise this positioning daily before any writing task until automaticity is achieved.

Activity 2: Pencils and grips

All students should start out using a pencil that is easy to grip, erasable and light in weight. There are also some pens on the market which are erasable. Be careful, though. The ink in those pens fades due to heat brought on by the friction produced when using the 'eraser' part. But heat can come from other sources. I once had a student who used a pen like that. He took great care to do all his notation and homework in a big A4 book. He left that book on the dashboard of his mother's car one day in the sunshine, and when he brought the book to the lesson and opened it up, all his work had disappeared!

Pencils are good for handwriting practice. I myself used to press very hard on the paper in an effort to control my handwriting. It wasn't until I went to a school in the Netherlands that I encountered fountain pens. In continental Europe, fountain pens were a standard writing implement back then and I fell in love with them from the first moment I used one. The softness and relative weakness of the metal nib forced me to press less heavily on the paper and as a result I had to consciously develop neater handwriting by means other than pressure.

1. Practise opening and closing the middle finger and thumb. These will form the grip on the pencil.
2. Practise holding a pencil and using the muscles of the finger and thumb ONLY to move the pencil back and forth.

Activity 3: The lines and the direction in which we read and write

In English, we read and write from left to right. At the beginning of every handwriting lesson, it is a good idea to orient students to this fact. I have a large whiteboard on the wall of my practice with arrows along the top going from left to right, to which I refer constantly.

It is also necessary to familiarise children with the lines on their page. Most primary schools provide special handwriting books with guidelines already printed in them, but it's important to establish names for these lines so that explicit instruction can take place.

There are three main points on the handwriting page that students need to be aware of. They are:

1. The bottom line. This is the line on which all the letters sit.
2. The top line. This is the line all tall letters reach towards. Try to encourage children not to actually touch the top line, as this will cause crowding and reduce clarity.
3. The middle line. This has different appearances depending on the handwriting book that children are working with but take care to establish where it is and what to call it. The shorter letters of the alphabet will reach to there and not past it.

Have students point to these three lines on their paper and say what each line is: 'Bottom, top, middle'.

Have them use their pencils to mark each line with a dot, saying the name of the line as they mark: 'Bottom, top, middle' (Figure 22.1).

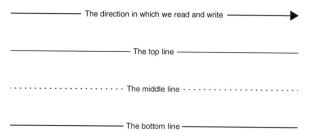

Figure 22.1 Handwriting lines

Activity 4: The clock face

I have a huge clock on my practice wall with very clear numbers on it. When handwriting is our focus, I have students point to various numbers on the clock to orient themselves to start and end points for letters. The magic number for all letters containing curves is the number 2.

There are certain letters that begin at 2 on the clock. The lower case ones are:

a c d f g o q s

The upper case ones are:

C G O Q S

All other letters begin with lines.

At first, students practise big circles, starting at 2, going up and back towards 12 and coming back to 2. They can do this by tracing with their fingers on a big clock and writing it on their imaginary screens, both big and small, and tracing then writing with pencil on paper until they can do beautiful circles. This is harder than it appears, but mastery of this and of the letters containing circles helps to steer children away from reversals and makes them so much more legible.

It often helps to have them articulate what they are doing while they are practising: 'I start at 2, I go up through 12 and I come back up to 2.'

Activity 5: Letter parts

All letters contain one or more of the following parts. Practise each part separately and learn the language for each part.

1. Big circles start at 2 on the clock. (C G O Q S)
2. Small circles start at 2 on the clock. (a c d f g o q s)

3. Lines can begin at the top and go straight down to the bottom line. (B b D E F H h I J K k L l M N P R T t U W)

4. Lines can begin at the middle and go straight down to the bottom line. (i m n r u y)

5. Lines can begin in the middle and go past the bottom line. (g q y)

6. Tall diagonal lines can start at the top and go in the direction that we read and write. (V X)

7. Tall diagonal lines can start at the top and go against the direction that we read and write. (A)

8. Short diagonal lines can start in the middle and go in the direction that we read and write. (v w x)

9. Short diagonal lines can also start in the middle and go against the direction that we read and write to complete other letters. (v w x)

10. Short, horizontal lines go in the direction that we read and write. (e Z z)

11. Small dots go on top of i and j and at the end of sentences.

Only upper case Y is strange. It starts at the top with a horizontal line in the direction that we read and write but stops at the middle line and starts again at the top with a tall diagonal line against the direction that we read and write.

Practise the letters at first on the student's visualised screens, nice and big, learning the various words that describe the starting point and what comes next. Have them take turns to write letters in the air, using the language you have taught them. Move to large letters on paper and eventually to small ones.

When writing letters as a handwriting focus, naming the letters rather than attempting to connect them to the sounds they make in words will help avoid confusion. Introduce the terms *lower case* and *upper case* too, and talk about where upper-case letters are appropriate.

This is the explicit part, but nothing will take the place of daily practice. Children need to be given the opportunity to be prolific writers from day one.

A note on dysgraphia

We all have our strengths and weaknesses, and sometimes, forming letters on a page is a severe weakness for some children. In extreme cases, problems with letter formation and organising/expressing written information is caused by neurological impairment. This impairment is known as *Written Expression Disorder* or *Dysgraphia*.

Arbitrary 'pen licence' systems that discriminate against children with poor letter formation, regardless of cause, are frowned upon by this author and those of us in the field who have to deal with struggling children. It is a school's responsibility to establish good handwriting techniques from the very start, and it is also their responsibility to monitor and provide understanding and appropriate support for children who struggle with this. Pen licences occupy the same reprehensible territory as discouraging left-handedness, corporal punishment and reprimanding people who stutter.

CHAPTER 23

Teaching the alphabet

The first thing I ask children to do when they come to see me is tell me the alphabet. Inevitably I get a song, and sometimes a very beautifully sung one too, with lots of expression and tunefulness. But it's not the alphabet. What it is, is a string of notes with virtually meaningless speech sounds attached.

The song begins fairly distinctively, with all the letters separated out, but the middle letters often suffer from a bit of a collision, sounding something like 'Elmo pee' or what have you. The letter following <q> often sounds like <i> and sometimes we even get '<q i x>' instead of <q r s>. The grand finale usually reflects a surge in confidence, with '<w x y> ... AND ... <z>!' and even sometimes the 'Now I know my ABC, next time won't you sing with me' refrain. I then tend to burst into wild applause.

'Fabulous effort!' I say. 'Now I'm going to set you a new challenge. I want you to take some time over the next few weeks to learn the alphabet backwards. Yes, I really mean backwards! You might think that's impossible, but it's not. I'm going to show you some steps you can take to get there, and then your job is to master each step. Before you know it, you'll be able to say the alphabet backwards and you'll probably be the only person in your class who can do this.'

It seldom fails to intrigue them.

Intriguing or not, just a cute alphabet backwards party trick is not what I have in mind. Children often learn the alphabet as a stream of musical notes with no reference to the names the letters represent. Children also go through stages of alphabet knowledge. My middle daughter used to sing, 'a b c d e f g ... w dot ...' before she got the hang of the whole thing. All of this is fine, but we mustn't assume that all children will just implicitly grasp it.

At school, there is very little explicit teaching of each separate letter. Along with irregular verbs, this is something most children develop an understanding of independently, and schools move right along, leaving behind those who didn't.

Why do we care? The realisation that letters have names and exist in a specific order is useful for the following reasons:

- The world is alphabetised. From favourite songs to reference materials, from a wine list in a restaurant to a simple filing system at the office, alphabetical order matters.
- Knowledge of the alphabet helps bridge the gap between pre-reading and reading.
- Spelling out loud requires the rapid naming of alphabet letters in sequence. No one spells out their name to someone on the phone by sounding it out, 'My name is /l/-/ɪ/-/n/'. No, 'My name is <l>-<y>-<n>' is what we say.
- Naming the letters of the alphabet is important meta language when discussing spelling.
- Vowel letters can represent their alphabetic name, depending on various orthographic signals. Knowing the vowel names is therefore important.

In sum, a child will have a more solid foundation for reading and is likely to be a better speller if they properly know the alphabet. Later on, they will be able to use reference materials and alphabetised lists more efficiently.

The steps:

1. If the alphabet is known only as a song, praise this achievement.
2. The next task is to *learn the alphabet like a robot*. Instead of singing the song, children now have to learn to say the letters in sequence with a small pause in between each letter, especially at the troublesome areas. They also have to use a robotic voice, rather than a sing-song one so that transfer of this sequence takes place and the song, which is essentially a meaningless stream of sounds, is left behind.
3. With the robot alphabet, teach the child to not say the word 'and' any more. This word is not in the alphabet and needs to be extracted.
4. To help with this, children are given an alphabet chart and have to touch each letter and say the letter name from <a> to <z>. Distributed practice is ideal here – that is, short, sharp practice over a longer period of time. So perhaps at the beginning of short, daily literacy sessions is best.
5. The child moves from touching and saying the letters to writing the letters in the air and on paper. More details about air-writing can be found in the handwriting chapter. For the youngest beginners, writing is not introduced yet.
6. Make sure the concept of *beginning, middle* and *end* are known to the child and then play the Position Game. Say a letter name and have

the child locate the letter as quickly as possible on their chart, telling you whether the letter is close to the beginning, middle or end of the alphabet.

7. Play the Position Game with finer and finer grain, using the mind's eye instead of the alphabet chart and asking for clearer descriptions of exactly where the letters are.

8. Move from the Position Game to the Before and After Game, where you name a letter and the child has to rapidly call out the letter before and the letter after.

9. After all this, you can teach the backwards alphabet in seven steps using distributed practice techniques:

zyx

wvut

srqp

onm

lkji

hgf

edcba

Transition to the next stage

To maximise learning, it is advisable to help students transition to the next stage of literacy during these exercises. Nothing recommended here or in any good literacy program is done in isolation, but instead should form part of the weft and warp in the tapestry of skilled reading and writing.

There aren't many foundation classrooms that don't have an alphabet chart on the wall but these charts vary greatly in their usefulness.

The most common charts depict lower and upper case letters and a picture reminder of a common sound that the letter represents, e.g. A a and a picture of an apple next to it. Some charts have no pictures at all. Others have extremely elaborate pictures.

There is promising research which shows that simple embedded alphabet pictures facilitate letter–sound association. In one experiment, designed to ease the task of learning foreign alphabets, the authors concluded:

> *Embedded letters were mastered in fewer trials, were less frequently confused with other letters, were remembered better 1 week later, and facilitated performance in word reading and spelling transfer tasks compared to control letters.*

(Shmidman & Ehri 2010)

The Read-Write Inc. program is one such resource. The cards used to teach letters and sounds to children are double-sided. One side has a letter with a superimposed picture on it. For instance, the letter <d> is curled round a dinosaur. Instructions about how to write the letters also form the shape of the pictures.

Alphabet teaching checklist

The checklist in Figure 23.1 contains all the different ways of knowing the alphabet from simple to complex. New students in my practice have their entry point noted and each level checked off as part of their ongoing progress monitoring.

Task	Date started	Date mastered
Partial alphabet song		
Full alphabet song		
Full alphabet *like a robot* (with no 'and' in it)		
Reciting the alphabet and writing it in the air		
Reciting the alphabet and writing it on paper		
Position Game (gross) pointing to the chart		
Position Game (fine) pointing to the chart		
Position Game (gross) in the air		
Position Game (fine) in the air		
Before and After Game		
Backwards alphabet		

Figure 23.1 Alphabet teaching checklist

Reference

Shmidman, A., & Ehri, L. (2010). Embedded Picture Mnemonics to Learn Letters. *Scientific Studies of Reading*, 14(2), 159–82. DOI: 10.1080/10888430903117492

CHAPTER 24

Teaching phonological awareness

For typical learners, high quality literacy instruction will give sufficient practice in and development of phonological awareness (PA).

If a child is struggling with literacy, a good first step is to have their PA assessed. There are several good, reliable and cheap PA assessments available. A Google search will lead to them, though personally, I use the Sutherland Phonological Awareness Test (SPAT).

Presented here is a range of activities to help develop PA in students who need it. I use these in my practice regularly.

Special note:

My advice to anyone working with low PA students is to sit opposite them. That way they will be able to see your mouth, giving them a clearer view of the sounds you make during the session. It is also handy to have a mirror nearby so that students can see the shapes their own mouths are making when articulating sounds.

Kinaesthetic feedback

Speech-language therapists often teach students to *feel* what their mouths are doing while they make sounds as a way of correcting articulation and strengthening weak PA skills.

Developing students' conscious awareness of phonemes and syllables establishes a processing base that is reliable, self-monitoring and allows independence.

The first step is to make students aware of the *human articulatory mechanism*, i.e. the machine that makes sounds. This hollow tube from lungs to lips contains all the tools involved in the production of speech sounds.

Once the articulators (tongue, teeth and lips) are pointed out, students can then consciously produce phonemes and figure out what moved and how.

In linguistics, all speech sounds are categorised on the following basis:

Teaching phonological awareness

1. Voice: Is this a loud or quiet sound? Contrast /f/ and /v/. Both use exactly the same articulators in exactly the same manner, but the first sound, /f/, is made without vibration of the vocal cords. This can be called a quiet sound. The second sound, /v/, is made with the vocal cords vibrating. This can be called a loud sound.

The consonant construction chart in Table 24.1 shows which other sounds go in quiet and loud pairs.

2. Placing: What moved to make this sound? Contrast /p/ and /f/. /p/ uses both lips (bilabial), whereas /f/ uses the bottom lip and the teeth (labiodental).

The consonant construction chart in Tables 24.1 and 24.2 indicate which articulators are used in English speech sound production.

3. Manner: How was the sound produced? Contrast /p/, /s/ and /m/. Which one exploded out of the mouth? Which one used friction, or hissing? Which one came through the nose? (/p/ exploded, /s/ used friction and /m/ came through the nose.)

Table 24.1 Paired consonant chart

QUIET	LOUD	PRODUCTION
/p/ (pig)	/b/ (big)	The air is stopped by the lips before coming out in a popping manner.
/t/ (ten)	/d/ (den)	The air is pushed out by the tongue being pressed against the ridge behind the teeth.
/k/ (kill)	/g/ (gill)	The air is pushed out between the back of the tongue and the roof of the mouth.
f// (fan)	/v/ (van)	The air is pushed out between the top row of teeth and the lower lip.
/θ/ (thin)	/ð/ (that)	The air is pushed out between the top row of teeth and the tongue.
/s/ (sip)	/z/ (zip)	The air is pushed through a narrow gap between the upper and lower sets of teeth. The air moves in a continuous stream. The lips are narrowed.
/ʃ/ (ship)	/ʒ/ (vision)	The air is pushed through a narrow gap between the upper and lower sets of teeth. The air moves in a continuous stream. The lips are pushed out and forward.
/tʃ/ (chill)	/dʒ/ (Jill)	The air is quickly pushed through a narrow gap in the upper and lower sets of teeth. The air moves in a quick burst. The lips are pushed out and forward.

Table 24.2 Unpaired consonant chart

/m/ (map)	The air is pushed out through the nose. The lips are pressed together.
/n/ (nap)	The air is pushed out through the nose. The lips are open and the tongue is pressed against the ridge behind the upper set of teeth.
/ŋ/ (sing)	The air is pushed out through the nose. The lips are open and the tongue is pressed against the back of the roof of the mouth.
/l/ (light)	The air is pushed past the tongue which lifts to meet the ridge behind the upper set of teeth.
/r/ (right)	The air is pushed past the tongue which is raised and flexed towards the back of the mouth.
/w/ (wit)	The air is pushed past the lips which form a tight circle.
/h/ (hit)	The air is forced through a narrow channel far down the hollow tube, in a breathing manner.
/ʍ/ (whip)	The air is pushed forcefully through rounded lips, rather like the sound made when blowing out a candle. Many accents of English have merged this sound with /w/.
/j/ yes	The air is pushed through a narrow gap between the tongue and the roof of the mouth. The lips are pulled back.

The consonant construction charts also show the various ways in which English speech sounds are produced.

Consonants not in pairs

The final five consonants in this chart (l, r, w, h and wh) are slightly more tricky. This is because they act like consonants in that some turbulence is produced, but the obstruction in the tube is minimal compared to other consonants.

Vowels

Vowel sounds are also categorised according to placing and manner, but the difference is that they are all voiced and all unobstructed. This means that they are produced with an open vocal tract, i.e. no tapping, hissing, exploding, etc.

The vowel construction chart in Table 24.3 shows the ways in which English vowels are produced.

Vowel construction

Vowels in the majority of accents of English fall into four broad categories. Table 24.3 lists vowel sounds in Standard English. Scottish and American varieties would not include vowels plus <r>.

Table 24.3 Vowel construction chart

Manner	Explanation	Sounds	Example words
ROUNDED	The lips are not wide open and not pulled back, but pushed forward to varying degrees	/ɒ/ /ɔ:/ /ɜ:/ /ʊ:/ /ʊ/	got law her boot put
UNROUNDED	the lips are not wide open and not pushed forward but pulled back, to varying degrees	/e/ /ɪ/ /i:/	get sit tree
OPEN	the lips are wide open and not pulled back and not pushed forward	/æ/ /ʌ/ /a:/	bat gum bar
DIPHTHONGS	the vowel sound begins rounded, unrounded or open but ends elsewhere	/eɪ/ /ju:/ /aɪ/ /əʊ/ /ɔɪ/ /aʊ/	day due die goat boy cow

Activity 1: Identifying the articulators

Show the articulatory mechanism picture (Figure 24.1) and have students discover the parts involved in producing speech sounds. The parts are:

- lungs
- trachea (the hollow tube)
- larynx (vocal cords or voice box)
- tongue
- teeth
- lips

Watch out!

Sound is bounced off other mouth parts, including the hard and soft palate (the roof of the mouth) and the nasal passages. These are not the moving parts, they are the walls of the hollow tube. We are mostly interested in the moving parts, as they are most perceptible to students for the simple reason that they are moving.

Activity 2: Loud or quiet?

Have students locate and feel their vocal cords for the following sounds:

/m/ (loud)
/æ/ (loud)

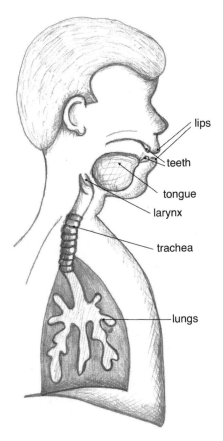

Figure 24.1 The human articulatory mechanism

/i:/ (loud)
/f/ (quiet)
/p/b/ (quiet /loud)
/t/d/ (quiet /loud)
/k/g/ (quiet /loud)

Their job is to tell you whether the sounds are loud or quiet. They can figure it out in a range of ways:

- placing fingers on throat and feeling for vibration
- covering the ears and feeling the sound through the skull sinuses if the sound is voiced
- deciding, in the case of pairs, which one they would use to wake a sleeping parent or teacher

Watch out!

This activity relies on two very important factors:

- That the teacher models the sound correctly, so that voiceless sounds are not artificially voiced, e.g. saying 'puh' for /p/. That's two sounds. The sound /p/ is articulated in the same way as the last sound in 'tap'.
- That the student copies the sound correctly. Some individual instruction might be necessary at first and those who have articulatory difficulties may need specialist intervention from a speech-language therapist.

Activity 3: Feeling the alphabet

Show each letter of the alphabet and guide the students into feeling whether the sounds most commonly associated with each letter are:

- quiet/loud
- made moving tongue, teeth or lips
- made with obstruction or no obstruction

NOTE: All vowels are loud and produced with no obstruction. Their difference is in the shape of the lips, the position of the tongue and the degree to which the mouth is open or closed.

This activity can be expanded beyond the alphabet letters and into the additional sounds and letter combinations as the students progress, e.g. <sh>, <th>, <ng>, etc.

Specific uses in literacy instruction

Once students have had some practice in identifying the different ways their mouths make sounds, this information can then be used to establish and correct reading and writing.

When reading aloud, if a child mistakes one sound for another, or cannot decode a letter, or omits a letter, for example, reading 'tee' for *tree*, take the following action:

1. Cover the word. Don't let them look back down at the word. That didn't work the first time. You are now going to get them to use a different system from their visual system to correct the word.
2. Ask, 'When you said *tee*, what did your mouth do right after the /t/?' (It made a smiley vowel sound, /i:/)

3. Uncover the word and point to the letter after t.
4. Ask, 'What do you see?' (/r/, which is a loud sound and requires the tongue to lift and curl towards the back of the mouth)
5. Say, 'Now say the word by tapping your tongue, then curling it back and *then* making the smiley vowel sound'.

When correcting spelling, point to the word and say:

1. That would say 'tee', but the word we want is *tree*.
2. In the word *tree*, what does your brain tell your mouth to do after your tongue taps? (It tells my tongue to lift and curl towards the back of my mouth.)
3. So what symbol matches that curled-back /r/ sound? (<r>)
4. Write it here (point after the <t>).

Syllables

A syllable is simply a vowel sound, with various consonants clustered around it in different patterns. That's all there is to it. If you want children to read and spell syllables accurately, then the best starting point is the knowledge that vowel sounds are central to syllables.

This section offers some techniques for counting syllables for reading and spelling.

For reading

Assuming that a child has been taught the basic sound–symbol code, they can start to apply that knowledge to words with more than one syllable.

This can be introduced by demonstrating a syllable counting technique on the board using the following dialogue:

TEACHER (Writes *tiger* on the board): Let's decode this word using a new system. Words can get very long, so sounding them all the way through all at once can sometimes be too much for your memory. Instead, we're going to learn how to quickly and easily break words into parts. We'll start slow, but with practice, you will be able to do this automatically. This will also help you with your spelling.

Mark the vowels that you see. (Student puts dot under each vowel, or vowel digraph, if you have taught these.)

For each dot, we know we have a syllable. So two dots equal two syllables. Vowels are like magnets and attract consonants to them, especially at the beginning of syllables. So knowing that, if you were to put a line in between the two syllables in this word, where would you put it?

STUDENT: After the <i>.

TEACHER: So now we have two syllables: *ti-* and *-ger.* Sound each one out and then put the word together.

NOTE: The dialogue above is a simple example. I would recommend explaining that the first syllable is also an open syllable and therefore the vowel is more likely to say its alphabet name rather than the common sound associated with it.

Watch out!

There is a practice called *toxic morphology* (Millar 2017) doing the rounds at schools right now, where well-meaning teachers coach students into 'chunking' words along nonsensical lines. When I see or hear the word 'chunking', I get a little suspicious.

Toxic morphology is the practice of encouraging students to look for 'little words inside big words' that have no meaningful relationship to one another. Just because there's a *meow* in *homeowner,* doesn't make possessing a house anything to do with cats! Tricia Millar from *That Reading Thing* says:

> *It's especially counterproductive to split a grapheme like <ear> in search-*
> light *to point out a familiar but unrelated word. To avoid adding an unneces-*
> *sary layer to the task of spelling, use morphemes accurately and only when*
> *they aid memory. Never ask your students to look for things like* hen *in* then,
> eat *in* weather, *or* act *in* fractional.

For writing

Most students learn to identify syllables through the mere act of clapping. Some with low PA, however, need more explicit instruction.

Zipped lips

Some students confuse phonemes with syllables. At first, a child asked to count the syllables in a word will often count the phonemes instead. Here is an example:

TEACHER: Count the syllables in *window.*

STRUGGLING STUDENT: /w-ɪ-n-d-əʊ/, five.

The following technique helps take the focus off phonemes and put it onto syllables instead. Have students do the following steps:

1. Say the word out loud.
2. Now pretend your mouth is zipped shut and say the word again.
3. Feel the impulses come through your nose.
4. Count the impulses with your fingers as you go along.

Watch out!

When doing this counting exercise, it helps to warn the students if there are 'collapsing syllables'. Words such as *Wednesday*, *dictionary* and *interesting* have syllables which you have to spell, but which you often don't hear in speech: 'wens-day', 'dic-tion-ry', 'in-trest-ing'.

Talk about collapsing syllables and how it's important to learn the word both for writing 'wed-NES-day' and for reading 'wens-day'.

Manipulating sounds in words

Phonemic awareness is a major branch of PA. It is the ability to perceive the number, order, sameness and difference of sounds within words. A crucial skill in the development of phonemic awareness is the ability to segment, blend and manipulate phonemes in words.

In my practice, I use several tools to help with this. One of them is a game where students track changes in increasingly complex words using coloured tiles.

Concrete sound manipulation

Some students will need extra help with sound manipulation. Additional to the visualising exercises earlier, students can also perform the same tasks with real, three-dimensional magnetic tiles.

Air-writing and tile-swapping activities are common practice in many language and literacy practices worldwide. The first time I saw this in action was at Lindamood-Bell Learning Processes in the 1990s. This company has expanded and developed these activities into extensive, research-based programs known as *Seeing Stars* and the *Lindamood Phoneme Sequencing Program (LiPS)*.

Reference

Millar, T. (2017). *That Spelling Thing: Lessons & Resources for Classroom Teachers in Secondary, College, Adult Education and Middle to Upper Primary*. Great Britain: Stalashen Press, 27.

CHAPTER 25

Teaching phonics

Phonics consists of showing people the written code and finding ways of helping them remember and apply it.

Where you draw the line in terms of the simple vs. the complex code is up to you. As a linguist, I prefer to have my students generate the code, rather than feed it to them on a plate, but my situation is somewhat different from a classroom teacher's.

The Snowman Game

When people come to see me, they have usually had some exposure to written language already, so I determine what that is and build on it. I also try to find out what they are being taught at school and how, and advocate for a code-based approach only until automaticity is achieved.

Sometimes this is incredibly hard. Most of my students end up in my practice because whole language has failed them. Most adults who work with them or hear them read use whole language and three-cueing methods to try to 'help' them. As a result, I get chronic guessers who blurt out random words rather than take the time to use the written code.

Apart from teaching the code, I also have to undo their guessing habits when reading aloud. For this, I use the Snowman Game (Figure 25.1). It's the same principle as hangman, but I don't find the image of a man hanging particularly fun.

My instructions go like this, 'I'm going to get you to read this story to me. If you get to a word you don't know, you need to sound out all the letters right from the first one to the last. Then, if you think you know the word, say the word. If you don't, I'll help you, but I can only help when you've sounded out every letter or letter team. If you guess the word by only looking at the first letter or thinking about what might make sense there, I get to draw a piece of my snowman. Don't let me draw that snowman!'

Figure 25.1 The Snowman Game

I have to make it fun and non-threatening, because in almost all cases, these children have been rewarded for guessing. Many of these children have large vocabularies too, so guessing has not been a problem until the volume and complexity of text increased. I am forced to pull the guessing rug out from under them and it's scary for them unless I'm very supportive.

It's a shame that parents have to spend money undoing what schools have taught their children, but the Snowman Game at least makes the process of phonic decoding to automaticity a little more bearable.

Vowels and vowel teams

Consonants, and the letters that represent them, are relatively simple. It doesn't take long to figure them out and use them well. Not so with vowels. There are five letters in the alphabet that represent vowel sounds and about 18–24 vowel sounds in the various accents of English. That's a mathematical problem right there. Two solutions have arisen:

1. Single vowel letters can represent several different vowel sounds (e.g. the letter <a> in *at, paper, bath, ball, swan*, etc.).
2. Single vowel letters can team up with other letters, namely other vowels (<oo>, <oi>, <ee>) or a small set of consonants (mainly <r>, <w> and <y>), to represent certain vowel sounds.

I am not going to get into the nitty gritty of digraphs, trigraphs and suchlike here. I've seen many, many approaches to teaching these. As long as schools

are consistent and their efforts lead to fluent reading and writing in the short-
est time for the greatest number of children, the order and terminology is
secondary. If, however, schools and school leaders prefer to pick phonics programs apart with spurious 'exceptions' or odd arguments about terminology,
they've missed the boat.

The chart below shows how they are set out in my practice (Figure 25.2). Please
bear in mind that I teach children with non-rhotic accents, i.e. they do not pronounce the letter <r> after vowels. For Scots, like me, or American, Canadian,
Irish and Cornish people, there are only two Beautiful Babies, not three.

Each single letter and digraph on the chart is a moveable magnetic tile. I
scramble them up on the board and the children learn to reassemble the tiles
systematically, one column at a time. Each tile leads to the next.

Embedded in this chart is information about orthographic signals, statistical
likelihood of spelling patterns, allowable word endings, etc. We refer to all of this
as the lessons proceed. Once they have reassembled the tiles, students then touch
each one in order and say the most common sound associated with that tile.

Column 1

The first column, titled 'Single vowels', consists of the five vowel letters in
English. Students touch each one and say the five most common sounds of
those letters – that is, the vowel sound in the words *bag, beg, big, bog* and
bug, respectively.

Column 2

Then I explain that the letter <e> is often used as a signal in words, to remind
us that a vowel is saying its name. It can even be separated from the vowel by

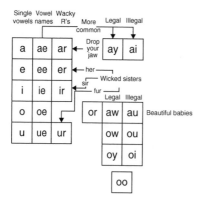

Figure 25.2 The vowel chart

one consonant letter; a combination that some like to call a 'split digraph'. I don't use that term, and *Spelling for Life* will tell you why.

So the second column reads like the vowel sound in the words *day, see, tie, toe* and *due* respectively. However, the sound /eɪ/ is not usually spelled with the pattern <ae>, so an arrow comes out of that tile and leads to the more common spelling of this sound: the two-letter /eɪ/ you may use at the end of words (legal) and the two letter /eɪ/ you may not use at the end of words (illegal).

Column 3

When you add the letter <r> to a single vowel, it alters the sound of the vowel. I call them *Wacky <R>s*, in that <r> makes the vowel go 'wacky'. Some call it *Crazy <R>*, some call it <R>-controlled vowels. Again, I don't care, as long as you are consistent. If you speak with a rhotic accent, these teams represent two phonemes, vowel + <r>. The vowel sound is still altered by the placement of the <r>.

The first team, <a:>, requires a vowel sound made with a relatively wide vocal tract. Therefore, the reminder 'drop your jaw' is there as a prompt.

There are three vowel + <r> combinations that sound the same, called the Three Wicked Sisters (see *Spelling for Life*). They are the <er> of *her*, the <ir> of *sir* and the <ur> of *fur*. Their alphabetic order is also their order of commonality.

Additional vowel teams

If you're English or Australian, the fourth Wacky R can be pulled aside and linked to the other two common spellings of this sound. They are called the Beautiful Babies, because when you see a beautiful baby, you make an 'awww' sound. Their spelling is legal <aw> and illegal <au>. Illegal letters are not permitted word-finally in English words.

Another legal/illegal pair is positioned below, i.e. <ow> (of *cow*) and <ou> (of *out*). Below that is the last legal/illegal pair, the teams <oy> and <oi>.

Finally, there is the double <o> team. This again is accent-dependent (I make no distinction between words spelled with <oo>, such as *boot* and *foot*, but many do). However, if you want to help the 20% who struggle with spelling, please let me offer you a tip:

PLEASE DO NOT TEACH the letter <o> as representative of the sound /uː/. PLEASE. It is misleading. Granted, there are some very common words where <o> is representing /uː/, but *please* for the sake of children who then use it to represent every /oo/ sound they hear, stop making it a legitimate choice for them. For example, because students are taught this, I see them write 'bot' for *boot*, 'son' for *soon* and 'tro' for *true*. Please don't teach this as a 'spelling choice'.

Here is a word family where <o> says /ʊ:/ in most accents:

to, two, do, who, lose, move, prove, shoe, canoe

Teach the family. Everyone wins.

The letter <o> represents the sound /ʌ/ in many more words than the sound /ʊ:/:

mother, brother, other, love, shove, above, monkey, money, honey, monk, front, won, come, some, etc.

Teach that family too, but please don't offer the letter <o> as an / ʊ:/ sound, it makes children spell badly.

Phonics and sight words

The process of sight word reading is different from that of using letters and sounds to decode unknown words. In sight word reading, the words are read from memory, not from decoding and blending operations, because the words are familiar. As a result, the act of reading them is carried on by memory processes, not by decoding processes. (Gaskins et al. 1996)

Despite anti-phonics claims that English is not a phonetic language, the truth is that over 85% of words can be phonically read and written using the alphabetic code. A further 10% can be spelled correctly using morphology and etymology and fewer than 4% could be classed as truly irregular (Moats 2010). Those who wish to argue against this, bring in small, common words as an example (*was, said, other*). This is a straw man.

In some cases, the pronunciation of small, common words has changed more rapidly than their spelling. It still doesn't make them hard to teach. Stating the opposite says more about a teacher's skill than the words themselves.

By sight words for reading, we mean words that can be instantly recognised without using phonic clues. This does not mean, however, that children should not place them in orthographic memory through orthographic mapping. They can and still should. The following technique shows how to do so with the Survival List.

Firstly, to learn a word as an immediately recognisable unit, a person has to see that word a certain number of times. That number varies per word and per individual. Therefore, a good method of placing a word in the long-term memory is frequency of exposure. This is where flashcards can be helpful, especially if the child is still at the decodable reader stage and isn't quite reading for pleasure yet.

The difference between using flashcards effectively and ineffectively, however, is how the words got onto the flashcards in the first place and what they look like when they're there.

Teaching of words on the Survival List must not precede the teaching of letter–sound correspondences. They must also be taught by identifying unusual patterns within them. For absolute clarity, 'unusual patterns' does not mean 'the shape of the word if you draw a box around it'. It refers to letter-sound correspondences that occur in only a few examples in the language.

I keep track of unknown words for spelling and reading for all my students. They are two completely different lists. The words for spelling are collected through assessment of the Survival List and harvested from written tasks. When students make errors in dictation or composition, it is not enough to simply ask them to re-spell those words and learn them by rote. Instead, I note the patterns that were troublesome for them and put those words into families of related words wherever possible.

Their homework is to say the words in their columns two ways, first for spelling, then for reading. The 'for spelling' part consists of them sounding each letter or letter team in sequence, including silent letters. This helps them to map those words and sequences into their orthographic lexicon.

The 'for reading' part is saying the whole word. Saying a word for spelling always precedes saying it for reading. The two ways of saying each word are practised together as much as possible.

Putting their words on flashcards for practice outside our lessons takes place in a certain way. Let's say I want the student to practise reading the word *shout*. I often hear this pronounced as 'shot' or 'shut' because it contains one of the most difficult digraphs, the letters <o> and <u>, forming the sound /aʊ/. Here is the dialogue:

TEACHER: Let's look at this word. I'm going to write it out for you on this card and we'll mark the tricky parts. What are they?

STUDENT: The <sh> digraph and the <ou>.

TEACHER (marks those parts by underlining the <sh> and the <ou>): Let's say it for spelling.

STUDENT (saying the sounds): /ʃ/-/aʊ/-/t/

TEACHER: And for reading?

STUDENT: *Shout.*

Giant steps, baby steps

This is an ideal opportunity to recruit parents and peers.

Once you have a pile of words on cards, you can start playing with them. The size of the card should be about 10cm x 15cm. Just make sure the words can be seen from up to 10m away.

Have your student stand about 10m away. Mix up the cards and show them the first one. If they say it instantly, they get to take a giant step towards you. If they have to sound it through, using the phonic prompts that you've marked on the cards, they get to take a baby step.

When the student reaches you, they get a reward (make it small as they'll want to keep playing) and then they go back to the start. You can make it fun by pretending to be really scared that they're coming to get you.

Keep replacing the words they've mastered with new words. You can even create three levels: slow, medium and fast. In my practice, my students name the slow, medium and fast cards after animals, so the slow ones are turtles or snails, the medium ones are horses or rabbits and the fast ones are cheetahs or falcons.

NOTE: This exercise is a *supplement* to phonics, not a replacement. Its purpose is to increase exposure to phonically decoded words once they have been decoded and the patterns have been explicitly taught and noted.

Writing lessons

At first, phonics lessons require scaffolding to help students make the transition from speech to print. In my practice, I begin by using coloured magnets and letter tiles to help with this mapping process.

Let's take the word *play*.

We begin by going to the action area on the whiteboard. Here is the dialogue:

TEACHER: Let's look at the structure of the word *play*. First, place a coloured tile for every sound your mouth makes when you say that word.

STUDENT (simultaneously placing coloured tiles): /p/-/l/-/eɪ/.

TEACHER: Good. Now, the first sound is usually the easy sound. What sound?

STUDENT: /p/.

TEACHER: Okay, locate and place the letter that matches the /p/ sound (student does so). What's the next sound?

STUDENT: /l/ (locates and places the letter <l>).

TEACHER: What's the next sound?

STUDENT: /eɪ/.

TEACHER: Good, that's the vowel saying its name. Go to the vowels and locate the letter.

STUDENT (points to letter): This one.

TEACHER: Unless it's got a signal to make it say its name, that letter alone says /æ/. How do vowels say their names?

STUDENT: Using the letter <e>, like in the next column.

TEACHER: Great. So we have the letters <ae>. But why is there a line coming out of the top of these letters?

STUDENT: To remind us of the more common spelling of this sound.

TEACHER: Good, follow the arrow. What have you got?

STUDENT: Legal /eɪ/ and illegal /eɪ/.

TEACHER: Good, look at where you will be placing this pattern. Is it at the end or inside the word?

STUDENT: At the end.

TEACHER: So is it more likely to be legal or illegal /eɪ/?

STUDENT: It has to be legal (brings letters <ay>).

TEACHER: Say it two ways, first for spelling, then for reading.

STUDENT (Touching and saying): /p/-/l/-/eɪ/... *play*.

Once the word is practised for spelling and reading on the board (Figure 25.3), I put the letter tiles back and ask the student to carry the word in their memory back to their desk and write it in their exercise book, saying it for spelling while they are writing. If they forget, we repeat the tile process.

We do this with several words each lesson and set saying the words for spelling and reading as homework.

Several systematic synthetic phonics programs model spelling for students by holding up a finger/fingers for each phoneme and having them map spelling patterns onto each one. There are still others who use Elkonin Boxes (see Glossary) to do this kind of mapping.

I also use these techniques, but the coloured magnetic tiles at the board are a good half-step towards those slightly more difficult frameworks.

Teaching syllables with phonics

The procedure above is used for single syllable words. Multisyllabic words can still be learned using structural work with tiles, etc., but each syllable needs to be clearly laid out within the action area and on a straight line. The student has to ensure that there is a vowel on each line, as a bare minimum.

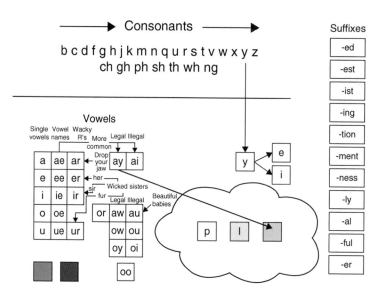

Figure 25.3 Writing lesson whiteboard

In the next chapters, we will look at some techniques for teaching syllables using phonics and morphology to help increase fluency and vocabulary.

References

Gaskins, I. W., Ehri, L. C., Cress, C., O'Hara, C., & Donnelly, K. (1996). Procedures for Word Learning: Making Discoveries about Words. *The Reading Teacher*, 50, 312–27.

Moats, L. C. (2010). *Speech to Print: Language Essentials for Teachers*, 2nd Ed. Baltimore, MD: Paul H. Brookes.

CHAPTER 26

Teaching fluency

Synthetic phonics is a method which teaches letter sounds and their associations in print. It then teaches blending the sounds together to form whole words. But what happens next? How does that translate to fluent reading and writing with comprehension?

Practice and opportunity to use new skills is the key. Again, this requires intelligent scaffolding, building from small components to larger ones. Unintelligent scaffolding would be encouraging the use of meaning or picture clues in an effort to bypass phonic decoding. It is wasted effort and not sustainable.

Should finger pointing be allowed?

To my great dismay, I have seen message boards and instructional materials that discourage the use of finger pointing when reading. I've heard it argued that teachers should only let children point at words while they read them for a certain time period and then they should start to discourage and/or forbid this use. Some say it slows a reader down and gets in the way of 'making meaning'. There is no evidence to support this view.

I regard myself as pretty literate, but I still use finger-pointing to carefully read documents like contracts and technical literature. Most of us do. Karaoke machines are even kind enough to break words into syllables and highlight the letters as we follow along. Who are we to say to children that they cannot also have this support?

I find it astonishing that those who claim to adhere to 'child-centred' learning would do something so utterly arbitrary and unnecessary. Discouraging finger pointing will not lead to greater skill, only greater stress.

When hearing them read, have students point to the first letter of each word and slide their fingers along the page to the end of the word, saying the sounds as they do. Allow students to track words like this for as long as they need to.

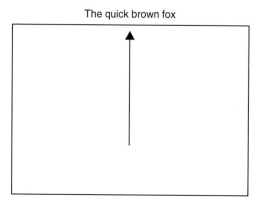

Figure 26.1 Arrow card for reading guidance

In some cases, finger pointing isn't enough. To keep the child's eyes on the words and on the correct line, I use a small piece of cardboard with an arrow in the middle of it, which points to the letters as the child moves it along the page (Figure 26.1). It also helps stop the next line interfering with the one the child is reading.

Correcting mistakes

When practising for fluency, it is a good idea to go through a set piece first for decoding. This is where children get the opportunity to merge their code-knowledge and sight word vocabulary with fluency practice. If a child comes across a word they do not instantly recognise, there are two helpful things you can do:

1. If the word can be sounded out using the patterns they know, encourage them to touch under each letter and sequence the sounds. You might model this for them at first by touching under each letter and saying, 'I'm going to help you with this word' and sound it through for them. At the end of sounding it through, say 'What word?' and praise them for saying the word. Get them to re-read the sentence that the word appeared in and check for understanding. Gradually fade this until they are independently sounding the words out.
2. If the word contains patterns they haven't been explicitly taught or that they haven't committed to memory, show them the pattern and sound it through for them. Make a note to teach or re-teach that pattern as soon as possible. Get them to re-read the sentence the word appeared in and check for understanding.

Never lose an opportunity to model good reading habits. Good readers fixate momentarily on each letter of each word. Fluency, expression and comprehension all begin here.

The performance piece

Many of my students are set homework where they have to practise reading a 'performance piece' before their next lesson. This is a sentence or sometimes a paragraph, depending on the age and stage of the student.

First we thoroughly decode the piece, noting patterns that haven't yet been explicitly taught or committed to memory. We also define any new vocabulary and punctuation, and once the piece is decoded, we talk about what the main idea is, we talk about any details within the piece and we give it a title.

So the order is:

1. phonic decoding
2. vocabulary
3. comprehension
4. fluency

Next, the student takes the piece away and practises until ready to perform. This usually takes a week or so.

The point is that fluent reading takes practice and, for some, heavy scaffolding before it's automatic. At first, students may try to memorise the piece, but given the correct complexity and length, they will have to decode. When they do that, they will be placing spelling patterns into their orthographic lexicon. Finding the correct performance piece is an art in itself, and one well worth developing.

This exercise goes alongside explicit, systematic code-based teaching. It does not form the backbone of the lesson, but instead demonstrates the purpose of reading practice. When there is too much emphasis on incidental teaching and memorisation of short passages or repetitive books, this is a problem, but as part of an overall routine, it lets the student showcase his or her new skills and hard work.

Resources

One of the best resources I've seen that directly targets fluent reading is *Reading Pathways* by Dolores Hiskes. The first section is especially useful to help students take the leap from phonic decoding to fluent reading.

This inexpensive little book contains a cumulative set of exercises to help build fluency in reading. It uses a pyramid-like structure to build graphemes into words. In 20 years of teaching children to read, I had never thought about teaching fluency this way. It is a work of genius.

Its focus is fluency, but it weaves the other pillars of literacy all the way through and is not shy about delightful, exciting vocabulary. I wish I'd had this book at the beginning of my career.

Writing aversion

I will now turn to the subject of writing fluency. Fluent writing is often talked about, but a little under-resourced. I have students enter my practice who exhibit absolute refusal to write, such is the school-induced trauma that writing has bestowed on them. The three great contributors to writing aversion, in my experience, are:

- arbitrary 'pen licences' that favour those with naturally neat handwriting and damn the rest to constant humiliation
- random 'spelling lists' to lift those with that type of memory to the top and heaven help anyone who needs explicit instruction
- the habit of keeping children in to complete written work when they should be having breaks

Instead, why not offer explicit, structured and scaffolded opportunities to write?

If you are ever at an education conference and see vendors trying to hawk their wares through a display of 'writing samples', be very suspicious. The mark of a good teacher or system is the output of their *bottom* students, not their *top* ones. I, and a great many people like me, learned to read and write through an entirely fortunate and unearned combination of genetic endowment, very early exposure to and instruction in print, and mountains of self-directed practice because *that is what I liked to do*. No teacher or program was responsible for this and I loathe the thought of someone out there claiming phony credit where it's not due.

If you want to impress me and the thousands of other people in the field who understand the difference between implicit and explicit learning, show me your worst examples and tell me how you're going to fix that.

The 21 Day Writing Challenge

When children come to see me in my practice, they do so for an hour per week. That's 1/168th of their lives. This cannot be the only time they get opportunities to practise their new skills. I have to get them to keep pushing forward in the time that I don't see them.

To that end, I eventually place them on the 21 Day Writing Challenge. This is intended to help students establish the habit of writing. It's a challenge because writing is the apex of literacy. It requires every thought process involved in turning speech to print, along with motor control, posture, creativity, planning, linguistic knowledge and so on. It is one of the most complex and difficult things humans can do. If it's already a struggle at earlier levels of literacy, imagine what it must be like to have someone *demand* writing from you in the absence of tools that make sense and at the expense of your much-needed downtime.

It doesn't have to be this way.

A habit is a fixed way of thinking, through previous repetition, of a mental experience. There is a common myth that it takes at least 21 repetitions to form a new habit. The actual number numbers varies greatly in the literature (Lally, Jaarsveld, Potts & Wardle 2010), but 21 days is a good starting point for these exercises.

Children whose literacy is developing in a typical manner form habits that help them continue to progress and become increasingly proficient. They scribble, write, take notes and copy text in many different contexts. For instance, how often have you seen children drawing pictures and putting words into the mouths of their characters? Have you ever received notes from children? These are all habits that typically developing children have. Habitual writing has a 'multiplier effect' on children's skills. The act of writing or copying is something they do with frequency and those rich in those habits get richer, while the poor get poorer.

Children who struggle with literacy form habits to avoid practice or miss out on opportunities to form habits that help them progress. This happens because they are stuck at the lower levels of literacy acquisition (i.e. phonemic awareness and phonics). The act of writing or copying is something they avoid or do infrequently.

This challenge is a way of allowing the students to access the multiplier effect that habitual writing gives. It is not intended to take the place of formal, expert intervention, but instead, is designed as a scaffolded booster to help form the habit of writing.

The process

Students are given an exercise book and a Challenge Chart. Each session, they choose an activity from the Chart, they do the activity and then they record it on the chart. By 'session', I mean a time when the child and a teacher or carer has 10–15 minutes to sit down and do some writing focus.

There are three levels:

1. Copying

Students copy from a given text (usually no more than 5 sentences). If possible, they are timed and the goal is to beat their time *but* to remain as accurate as possible. Their accuracy score is derived from the total number of words minus the total number of errors and expressed as a percentage.

This is the most heavily scaffolded activity. It helps to develop their orthographic lexicon and gives them exposure to good quality writing and punctuation. The same text can be used multiple times to help establish the speed score.

2. Dictation

Students have a passage read to them and must write this down. This is not timed but still requires an accuracy score.

Errors are recorded and stored for specialist work in their spelling books. For instance, if the child misspells *write* as 'rite', this information is passed on to the person in charge of building the student's personal word family list during specialist intervention. The pattern *silent <w>* can then be taught and other words in that family can be listed and practised together, e.g. *wrong, wrist*, etc.

3. Composition

The student chooses a word (either a misspelled one or one from their word family list) and orally composes a sentence.

The teacher asks if there are any words that they need help with and gives assistance where due. The student writes out the sentence by hand and edits it. Attention to capitals and punctuation is a must.

Some helpful tips:

- The columns in the Challenge Chart should be limited to having five full at any one time. Once a column reaches five full spaces, it is no longer a choice until the other two columns have caught up. This prompts the student to do the harder tasks as well as the easier ones. If this weren't enforced, children would likely choose copying as their only activity and the harder parts wouldn't get done.

- Choose texts that are approximately one year below grade level for copying. These can consist of several sentences and can be re-copied in an effort to raise speed and accuracy scores.
- Choose texts that are approximately two years below grade level for dictation.
- Give feedback after every exercise and talk about strategies to aid improvement. Harvest difficult words and patterns and work them into subsequent lessons, always paying attention to morphology, etymology and word meanings (Figure 26.2).

Cursive handwriting

To teach or not to teach cursive? There is much research to indicate the benefits of explicit handwriting instruction (Dinehart 2014), but where do we draw the line? Does cursive writing only benefit those who have the motor skills to make it legible? Should we be satisfied with manuscript handwriting and let technology take over?

Again, I find myself considering the 20% who struggle. Insisting on cursive writing while they are still coming to grips with sound–symbol associations seems odd. Odder still is the teaching of beginning handwriting that incorporates flicks and upswings and open letters in anticipation of cursive writing

Days	Copying	Dictation	Composition
1			
2			
3			
4			
5			
6			
7			
8			
9			
10			
11			
12			
13			
14			
15			
16			
17			
18			
19			
20			
21			

Figure 26.2 21 Day Writing Challenge chart

later up the track. Nearly every student who comes to see me is impaired in some way by this unnecessarily complex script.

The Spalding system teaches two very distinct stages of handwriting: the manuscript, followed by the cursive. The manuscript letters are complete in themselves with no openings where openings shouldn't be and no extraneous flicks. These are learned later on as whole components and bolted onto stably formed manuscript letters once manuscript fluency is achieved.

This is a system that I can support.

References

Dinehart, L. (2014). Handwriting in Early Childhood Education: Current Research and Future Implications. *Journal of Early Childhood Literacy*, 15(1), 97–118.

Lally, P., Jaarsveld, C., Potts, H., & Wardle, J. (2010). How Are Habits Formed: Modeling habit formation in the real world. *European Journal of Social Psychology*, 40(6), 998–1009.

CHAPTER 27

Teaching vocabulary

Most people understand the definition of vocabulary, but writing it into a curriculum or doing positive, explicit things to raise vocabulary levels in students is not as clearly defined.

There are a few techniques I base any vocabulary work on in my practice, outlined below. Mostly, as a result of this, I want my students to understand three basic concepts:

1. Words exist in networks and families.
2. Words have histories and knowing these histories helps with spelling and connecting to other words with similar origins.
3. Words contain meaningful parts that can be learned and applied to other words to work out their meanings too.

This chapter offers some methods I use in order to get these ideas across and help expand my students' vocabularies. Some of the children who come to see me have vast vocabularies. The majority have been read to and extensively spoken to by their parents since infanthood and have a huge store of known words. Some, however, have language impairments that make it hard to learn new words, despite everybody's best efforts. Rather than try to rewrite a whole vocabulary program, the following lessons are for children who need some intensive teaching in basic vocabulary to help them catch up with the mainstream. Inevitably, all vocabulary lessons are interwoven with spelling, reading, etymology and morphology. How could they not be?

Morphology

I cannot lie; this is my favourite subject. I love the small, meaningful units of words (called morphemes) that give us the breadth and depth of language. There is so much information contained in a morpheme, it never ceases to amaze me. I am seldom shy about using the words *prefix*, *root* or *suffix* in my practice, no matter how young my students are. They should have those words from the beginning of their education and they should know a great many of them before they leave primary school.

On the whiteboard on my wall, I have some magnetic tiles onto which I've written common prefixes and suffixes. Prefixes are relatively easy to teach, so most of the time, I concentrate on suffixes.

The –ed suffix

One of the most common spelling mistakes I see in primary school children's writing is the misapplication of the –ed suffix (e.g. 'playd' for *played*, 'helpt' for *helped* and 'landid' for *landed*). In the absence of explicit teaching and/or not enough independent reading, these children often do not make the association with this suffix and its function as a tense marker. It can be mastered in reading relatively quickly, by connecting to oral language, but its spelling can dog students all the way through primary school. It can and should be tackled as early as possible.

To make matters worse, this suffix can be pronounced three different ways, according to the root that it's attached to. If the root ends in a loud (voiced) sound, the suffix takes on that noise and sounds like /d/. If the root ends in a quiet (unvoiced sound), the suffix takes on its quiet form: /t/. If the root ends in <d> or <t>, a schwa sound is inserted before the noisy /d/. This is to help pronunciation. If you try to say the root words plus –ed with mismatched voicing, it feels and sounds awkward.

Figure 27.1 is a quick reminder.

To start off, I introduce the concept of tense. My students need to understand that there is a past, a present and a future and that these concepts are expressed in language using certain signals. I do this with a simple timeline showing the past, present and future and some words we use to express that (Figure 27.2).

ROOT WORD	+	ENDING	=	SOUND
play		loud sound		loud /d/
help		quiet sound		quiet /t/
land		/d/ or /t/		/ə/ + /d/

Figure 27.1 –ed suffix sounds

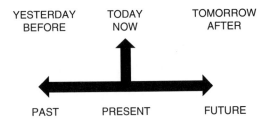

YESTERDAY   TODAY   TOMORROW
BEFORE   NOW   AFTER

PAST   PRESENT   FUTURE

Figure 27.2 Simple timeline

I then write the word *play* in the action area of the whiteboard and the following dialogue typically ensues:

TEACHER: This is the verb *play*. Today I like to play football. Tomorrow I will play football, and yesterday I ... what word?

STUDENT: Played.

TEACHER (pointing at timeline): Good. You changed the form of the verb *play* from present tense to past tense. When you spell that, you use the suffix –ed (place –ed suffix magnet after the word *play* to form *played*). Because *play* ended with a loud sound, the –ed suffix will also sound loud.

I then write the word *help* on the board:

TEACHER: This is the verb *help*. Today I like to help my family. Tomorrow I will help my family, and yesterday I ... what word?

STUDENT: Helped.

TEACHER (pointing at timeline): Good. You changed the form of the verb *help* from present tense to past tense. When you spell that, you use the suffix –ed (place –ed suffix magnet after the word *help* to form *helped*). Because *help* ended with a quiet sound, the –ed suffix will also sound quiet.

I then write the word *land* on the board:

TEACHER: This is the verb *land*. Today I land the plane. Tomorrow I will land the plane, and yesterday I ... what word?

STUDENT: Landed.

TEACHER (pointing at timeline): Good. You changed the form of the verb *land* from present tense to past tense. When you spell that, you use the suffix –ed (place –ed suffix magnet after the word *land* to form *landed*). Because *land* already had a <d> on the end, neither the quiet nor the noisy form of the –ed suffix will work here. It would make the word too hard to say.

So we have to put a vowel sound in between the end of the word and the suffix.

The student then writes the words *played*, *helped* and *landed* in their notebook, and practises other verbs with the –ed suffix through copying, dictation and composition.

The Yes/No Game

My board displays a set of suffixes at all times. To have students become familiar with the meaning and spelling of suffixes, as well as the effect they can have on root words, we play the Yes/No Game.

It starts by writing a simple word in the action area. We will use *call*.

TEACHER: This is the verb *call*. I call my dog. See how many suffixes you can add to *call* to make a new word. Every suffix you can add, put it in the *yes* pile on the right. Every suffix you can't add, put it in the *no* pile on the left.

The student then takes the first suffix, –ed, and puts it next to *call*.

TEACHER: What word?
STUDENT: Called.
TEACHER: Is that a word?
STUDENT: Yes.
TEACHER: Put the –ed suffix in the *yes* pile then.

Repeat the process, saying the complete word every time, even if it's not a real word, e.g. *callest, callist, calltion*, etc. This gives the student practice in pronouncing the suffixes and exposure to their spelling patterns (Figure 27.3).

TEACHER: You now have three new words that can be formed by adding suffixes to the root word *call*. What are the words?
STUDENT: *Called, calling, caller.*
TEACHER: Let's write them in your book.

Watch out!

You can play the Yes/No Game with hundreds of words, but there are some layers of complexity that you also need to teach explicitly with some

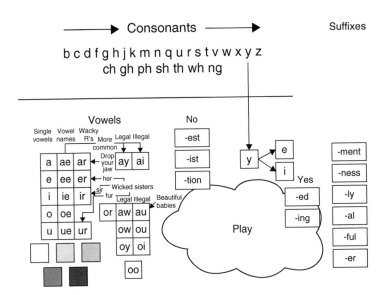

Figure 27.3 Yes/No Game whiteboard

root words. The first is when the root ends with Final Silent E. Let's take the word *hope*.

TEACHER: This is the verb *hope*. I hope it is sunny today. See how many suffixes you can add to *hope* to make a new word. Every suffix you can add, put it in the *yes* pile on the right. Every suffix you can't add, put it in the *no* pile on the left.

The student then takes the first suffix, –*ed*, and puts it next to *hope*.

TEACHER: What word?
STUDENT: *Hoped.*
TEACHER: Is that a word?
STUDENT: Yes.
TEACHER: Put the –*ed* suffix in the *yes* pile then.

Repeat the process, saying the complete word every time.

TEACHER: You now have three new words that can be formed by adding suffixes to the root word *hope*. What are the words?
STUDENT: *Hoped, hoping, hopeful.*
TEACHER: Before you write them in your book, I want you to do one more thing. This time, take the three suffixes that you have in the *yes* pile, and look at the first

letter. If the first letter is a vowel, keep it in the *yes* pile. If the first letter is a consonant, put it in the *no* pile. Now what do you have?

STUDENT: The suffixes *–ed* and *–ing* in the *yes* pile, and the suffix *–ful* in the *no* pile.

TEACHER: The ones in the *yes* pile are called vowel suffixes, for obvious reasons. What do you see at the end of the root word *hope*?

STUDENT: Final Silent E.

TEACHER: When you add a vowel suffix to a Final Silent E word, do you know what you have to do?

STUDENT: Drop the Final Silent E and then add the vowel suffix.

TEACHER: Correct. So make sure you do this when you come to write the new words in your book.

The second difficult scenario is when the root word ends with <y>. Let's take the word *happy*.

TEACHER: This is the adjective *happy*. We are very happy. See how many suffixes you can add to *happy* to make a new word. Every suffix you can add, put it in the *yes* pile on the right. Every suffix you can't add, put it in the *no* pile on the left.

The student then takes the first suffix, *–ed*, and puts it next to *happy*.

TEACHER: What word?

STUDENT: *Happyed*.

TEACHER: Is that a word?

STUDENT: No.

TEACHER: Put the *–ed* suffix in the *no* pile then.

Repeat the process, saying the complete word every time.

TEACHER: You now have four new words that can be formed by adding suffixes to the root word *happy*. What are the words?

STUDENT: *Happiest, happiness, happily* and *happier*.

TEACHER: Before you write them in your book, there's something you should know. When you add a suffix to a word that ends with <y>, a slight change happens. It doesn't matter if it's a vowel suffix or a consonant suffix, the change is the same regardless. We spell words with <y> at the end because the letter <i> is illegal at the end of words. The letter <y> comes at the end to solve this problem. However, when you add a suffix, the <y> is no longer at the end, so illegal <i> can return (rub out <y> and replace it with <i> and add the suffixes).

The student then writes the new words, with the adjustments, into their book.

Irregular past tenses

Another vocabulary deficit I see quite often is the ability to recall irregular past tenses. Many of my students need explicit teaching in this. Irregular past tenses are past tense verbs formed by a process different from simply adding the *–ed* suffix. For example, *run* becomes *ran*, *eat* becomes *ate* and *bet* remains the same as *bet*.

Because irregular past tense formation is mostly learned through observation, trial and error, typically developing children need little, if any explicit instruction in it. However, those with language disorders tend to lag behind in their knowledge of irregular past tenses.

The good news is, it doesn't seem to take very much instruction and practice in most cases to correct this. I use a simple list of common irregular verbs and go through it as part of the weekly lesson with all students. I say part of a sentence and they have to complete it with the correctly formed verb: 'Today I run, yesterday I …'.

If they don't know the word, I make a note and set it to practise for homework. I then check during the next session. I usually have a working list of five verbs for practice at a time.

There are many readily available irregular verb lists on the internet.

The days of the week

The days of the week are named after Norse gods and things in the sky. I teach this and get students to try and figure out which god/heavenly body each day refers to. Fortunately for us, there are many movies and TV shows these days all about the Norse gods.

Monday: Named after the moon. We lost an <o> somewhere in translation, but nobody minds.

Tuesday: That day belongs to Tyr, the one-handed Norse god of law and heroic deeds. His name changed through the ages and languages, from Tyr to Tiwar and finally gave us the *tue-* in Tuesday.

Wednesday: This day was named after the chief of all the gods – Odin. In old English, he was known as Woden, which gave us such an awkward spelling of Wednesday. It was Woden's day originally. The most effective way to remember that spelling is to clearly say the three parts: 'Wed-nes-day'.

Thursday: Children are always good at theorising who this day belonged to. Of course, the god of thunder – Thor! Thursday is Thor's day.

Spelling tip – There are two days of the week that have an /ɜ:/ sound in them: Thursday and Saturday. Both sounds are spelled with the *least* common spelling of that sound: the letters <u> and <r>.

Friday: Odin had a wife called Frigg, and Friday is her day. She was the goddess of wisdom.

Saturday: This day is often intuited by the students and is, of course, named after Saturn.

Sunday: Everyone knows this one. The sun gave us its name.

I have similar techniques for the months of the year and the cardinal and ordinal numbers, all of which can be found on my website and which should form the backbone of any good Survival List.

CHAPTER 28

Teaching comprehension

When students come to see me, they usually do so because they're struggling with reading and writing. What they have learned at school hasn't been sufficient to allow them to keep up with the majority of their peers and it's my job to give them tools to improve and catch up (Figure 28.1).

They often come with psychological reports which tell me about the underlying strengths and weaknesses, e.g. processing speed and working memory.

Reports or no, the first thing I do is measure their spelling ability, their reading and writing fluency, assess their handwriting, their alphabet knowledge and their comprehension.

This gives me a snapshot of the level they are working at, the level we need to work towards, and the kind of things they need to know and practise.

Most of them can't read anything fluently at their grade level, but the majority *can* answer grade-appropriate comprehension questions well if I read the story *to* them. A small percentage, however, also have difficulty with this and it becomes my job to help them comprehend better. It's not a job I relish, to be perfectly honest with you.

When good comprehenders can't read fluently it's a relatively easy task to give them the skills to catch up. This can sometimes look miraculous and it sometimes happens very quickly. There is a lot of pleasure to be gained by helping someone become a reader.

Helping people become better spellers is harder, but it's also satisfying to watch their skills improve and to watch them gain an understanding of the structure of words.

Helping people to comprehend what they read and hear is a long, slow process and the changes in students' skills are not as dramatic and detectable as reading and spelling progress.

The best training I have done on the subject is the Nanci Bell Visualizing and Verbalizing course.

Figure 28.1 Australopithecene

I also use the *Visualizing and Verbalizing Stories* resource to informally measure decoding and fluency and comprehension in my practice. They come in a set of three and have nine sections. Each section contains twelve stories from foundation to grade eight. Each story is followed by four or five comprehension questions.

If I am not following the steps in the Visualizing and Verbalizing program, I still check for comprehension during oral reading with all my students. If they are reading the wonderful stories from Reading Pathways, as soon as we see our first full stop we pause and I ask questions like:

Who is this sentence about?
What are they doing?
What do they look like?
What do you think is going to happen?
What word told you that?

I let students go back and locate the information they need if they can't answer from memory.

When we are reading longer texts I do the same, although I also ask for suggested titles, as this is a way of locating the main idea and summarising what has been read.

In schools, when decoding is not a barrier, reading comprehension is reliant on certain cognitive skills and background knowledge. There is much talk in education circles about trends towards knowledge-poor curricula and it worries me.

This is all I have to say about comprehension. If children are explicitly and systematically shown the alphabetic code from the age of five and are allowed to practise it, if they are given explicit teaching in vocabulary and fluency and if their phonological awareness is assessed and addressed, comprehension develops alongside in the majority of cases.

Sure, children can be taught to be more critical in their thinking, more discerning in their opinion-forming, more adept at locating, recalling, inferring and summarising information, but if you want to make sure they can do that in response to things they are reading, then teach them to actually read the words.

Glossary

alphabetics An umbrella term for phonological awareness, print awareness, letter knowledge and phonics.

blend A sequence of two or more consonants within a syllable.

comprehension The ability to understand what is read or heard.

constructivism A theory of learning that states the obvious, i.e. that people learn by experiencing things, reflecting on them and constructing their own view of the world. The danger in an over-emphasis of the constructivist view is that it places content-rich, direct instruction at the bottom of the merit pile.

convergence A term in science to describe the action of several fields collaborating and coming to a universal agreement about certain phenomena.

decodable readers Series of books for beginning reading instruction that contain only the patterns that have been explicitly introduced, as a temporary scaffold for initial reading.

digraph A speech sound represented by two letters.

direct instruction A method of teaching which involves direct, explicit guidance in specific subject concepts to bring about mastery of the subject area.

Direct Instruction ('Big DI') A commercially available suite of teaching materials in multiple subjects based on direct instruction.

distributed practice A strategy which allows practice of newly learned concepts to take place in small bursts over a longer period of time, rather than in longer sessions.

dyslexia A problem in the language systems of the brain that interferes with the smooth conversion of speech to print or print to speech.

Elkonin boxes Named after psychologist Daniil Elkonin, these are a visual aid to segmenting words into sounds. One box represents one sound and may contain combinations of letters. This helps cement grapheme-phoneme correspondence. It is not to be confused with the whole word practice of drawing boxes around letters to memorise their shapes.

evidence-based practice The integration of the best available resources, the highest skill level possible and the most viable method of teaching the individual student.

fluency A combination of accuracy in word decoding, automatic processing and prosodic reading.

generative Using a limited set of rules to generate all possible examples. This term is used in linguistics to explain the ability to form grammatical sentences without ever having heard the sentences before. This process can also be applied to spelling and vocabulary.

inquiry based learning (a.k.a. *problem based learning*) An instructional approach in progressive education that claims to foster critical thinking and creativity, but in many cases, leads to a detrimental thinning down of content and knowledge.

instructional casualty A student who fails to progress at the expected rate due to poor teaching.

learned helplessness A psychological condition brought about by persistent, unpleasant failure, leading to an inability to attempt avoiding the unpleasantness, a feeling of no control and a lack of motivation to take any steps to change the situation. The person has been conditioned to think that there is no escape from the unpleasant situation and so has given up trying.

literate language The more formal, structured language of education and literature taught at school.

literature review A summary of information found in books and papers related to a certain field, with the purpose of establishing a research base.

morpheme The smallest possible meaningful unit in a word. This can be a prefix, a root or a suffix.

MSL Multisensory Structured Language A commercially available program offered by the Institute for Multisensory Structured Language Education.

multi sensory learning A method of teaching literacy that attempts to simultaneously engage multiple sensory pathways.

onset A part of a syllable that precedes the vowel sound.

orthographic lexicon The store of correct spelling patterns each individual possesses and can draw on in writing.

peer-review The process by which an author's work is viewed by experts in the same field to evaluate its quality. It is an important gold standard in science, but severely under-utilised in education.

phoneme The smallest possible unit of sound.

phonemic awareness The ability to perceive and manipulate individual sounds within words.

phonics A method of teaching people to read and write by showing them the associations between sound and print. There are various ways to do this and therefore various types of phonics.

phonological awareness (PA) A sensitivity to the sounds and sound patterns of language.

phonotactic constraints Rules governing the way syllables can be constructed in languages.

predictable readers Series of books for initial reading instruction that contain words that can supposedly be predicted from picture, context and/or repetition clues. Individual sounds in words and spelling patterns are ignored in predictable readers.

progressive education In opposition to 'traditional' education, progressivism favours 'hands-on', project and inquiry based learning. Progressive educators use words like 'problem solving', 'personalised learning', 'cooperative learning' and 'critical thinking' but can often get lost in this jargon, especially when it comes to teaching children to read and count.

qualitative assessment Assessment based on the world view of stakeholders rather than measurable factors.

quantitative assessment Assessment based on scores and measurable outcomes.

randomised, controlled trial (RCT) A scientific process which tests the validity of a hypothesis or method by observing treatment groups (who receive the treatment) and control groups (who do not). The participants in both groups are randomly selected and assigned to the groups.

replication The act of testing a hypothesis in a different lab and yielding the same results. If an experiment cannot be replicated, it is not considered valid.

research The act of testing a hypothesis and reporting findings. If a program is said to be research-based, it means that the central hypothesis within the program has been tested and shown to be valid, either through direct study of the program itself, or of the main techniques within the program.

response to intervention (RTI) A three-tiered approach to teaching and behaviour which emphasizes early identification and intervention for students before they fail or are excluded.

rime A part of a syllable that contains the vowel and any following consonants.

schwa A neutral vowel sound, made with all the articulators relaxed and appearing in unstressed syllables, like the final <a> in *banana*.

statistical learning A sensitivity that develops, through exposure to the language, about the likelihood of certain patterns.

syllable A unit of sound made with one impulse of the voice.

Three-Cueing System (a.k.a. the searchlight model) A whole language method of teaching reading by training students to rely on semantic, syntactic and what is termed visual or 'graphophonic' cues to get words off the page. It de-emphasises phonological processing in favour of 'meaning-based' strategies. It is disastrously ineffective for a large population of children.

traditional education The continuation of well-established methods of teaching. It includes rote-learning and memorisation, testing, grading and external motivation like points and prizes. It is well-established because it works effectively.

whole language A range of methods of teaching reading based on the disproven theory that learning to read is the same as learning to talk.

working memory The ability to hold and process immediate information.

Index

Index